Out of the Rabble

OUT OF THE
RABBLE

Ending the Global Economic Crisis by
Understanding the Zimbabwean Experience

DAVID CHIWEZA

iUniverse, Inc.
Bloomington

Out of the Rabble
Ending the Global Economic Crisis by Understanding the Zimbabwean Experience

iUniverse books may be ordered through booksellers or by contacting:

iUniverse
1663 Liberty Drive
Bloomington, IN 47403
www.iuniverse.com
1-800-Authors (1-800-288-4677)

Because of the dynamic nature of the Internet, any Web addresses or
links contained in this book may have changed since publication and
may no longer be valid. The views expressed in this work are solely those
of the author and do not necessarily reflect the views of the publisher,
and the publisher hereby disclaims any responsibility for them.

Any people depicted in stock imagery provided by Thinkstock are models,
and such images are being used for illustrative purposes only.

Certain stock imagery © Thinkstock.

ISBN: 978-1-4759-7385-3 (sc)
ISBN: 978-1-4759-7386-0 (hc)
ISBN: 978-1-4759-7384-6 (e)

Library of Congress Control Number: 2013902497

Printed in the United States of America

iUniverse rev. date: 3/19/2013

Contents

Table of Figures

Acknowledgements

I am most grateful to God the Almighty, Father of my Saviour Jesus Christ, and to God the Holy Spirit for a personal revelation of truth and for His love of all nations and all His people. Because He is the way, the truth, and the life, I have been particularly committed to the truth without favour. For the truth will set us free. How can we escape from the truth without being in bondage ourselves?

I am also grateful to the nation and people of Zimbabwe. This is the nest and beautiful garden God chose for me. It has given me all the lessons I need in life. I look back and appreciate every hardship, every circumstance, and every experience, for it has contributed to my understanding of my world and what the world could be.

There are many people I am indebted to, directly or indirectly, for their contribution, motivation, and inspiration. I am reluctant to mention each by name, merely because I do not want them to be guilty by association. Special mention though goes to my commander-in-chief and my former commanders in the armed forces, who raised me from a teenager through to my adult life. My greatest training and experiences came through the nurturing mirror of military life.

I am grateful to my pastors, present and past, for their spiritual input, counsel, prayers, teaching, and motivation. It has not been easy for me to go public and display my foolishness. Everybody has the fear of failure, but their message has been consistent: in order for humans to progress, there must be somebody prepared to make a fool of himself.

I am grateful to friends, the home group, the accountability group, and the Winning Team for their encouragement. What could I do without the warmth of their friendship, care, and support? To the founder, chairman, and members of Victory Business Fellowship, I am grateful to them for opening their platform to me. Their comments and support continued to ring in my mind, and because I wanted to do well for them, I was very motivated to finish the book.

To my family, thank you for your perseverance. This journey has been marred by strange happenings, tough economic conditions, and painful situations. It almost seemed as though I should not proceed with writing, but you carried me along. To my wife, Kumbula, and children, I say thank you.

To my editors and reviewers of my manuscript, I am grateful for all the comments and critique. Each of the reviews helped me clarify and improve on my content. They did a great job of trying to make an author out of a messenger.

Finally, I am grateful to this information age. Through it, I see that the economic struggles of people all over the world are common, and by implication, there is hope for a common solution. I dedicate this book to all seekers of truth and to all those affected by the global economic crisis. May there be revelation!

Introduction

The world economy is in a crisis. Europe is burning. People are on the streets. The powers are looking for answers. Everywhere from the United States to Europe to Africa, there is growing uncertainty over the future.

But in the middle of all this, some nations are thriving. As the world is being initiated to the reality of an economic crisis, the small African nation of Zimbabwe has lived it all in the last two decades. It is a crisis arising from the free-market tsunami that crashed into her economy. She went into a tailspin, but now that the tide is coming back on shore, understanding the Zimbabwean story provides answers to how the world can come out of its crisis.

Since 2008, the global financial crisis has spread throughout the Western world, from the United States to Europe. It has seen high levels of company closures and unemployment. Companies and individuals are in debt. Banks are sitting on poorly performing loans, and there has been a wave of housing foreclosures. A number of banks faced collapse, and governments doled out billions in bailout funds. The European Union responded with austerity measures, and they are coming down hard on a people accustomed to good living. EU's gritty leadership seems determined to end the crisis.

But everywhere, news headlines display a common word: a deep recession, a stubborn recession, and a recession that keeps coming back.

This is a paradigm shift. The West will have to do new things to address it. In all affected nations, financial solutions were thrown at the problems, in a move that was designed to stimulate the economy. Beginning in the United States, the bailout solution model was extended to the crisis-ridden Eurozone, where nations like Portugal, Greece, Spain, and Italy face similar problems. While the stimulus packages represent some form of market creation, can the West continue to throw money at the problem by creating artificial market conditions, without creating sustainable markets for their economies to grow?

As Greece moved into another round of bailout money, it became apparent that the Eurozone's austerity measures were not a permanent solution to the financial crisis. While the focus is on banking sector irregularities, this book draws the attention of readers to markets as the real battleground and cause of the financial crisis. It challenges the notion of a global financial crisis and claims that there is an element of dishonesty about the crisis; financial and banking executives are blamed when in fact they are also victims of a tough new paradigm. The real problem appears to be the loss of markets through the emergence of Asia as an industrial power on the world scene.

This book originated in a prediction I made on 10 April 2000.[1] In an e-mail to Bill Brown, the founder of Thinkers International, I foresaw the development of the global recession and the need for bailout packages, which has now been fulfilled. In my communication to Brown, I predicted that the next global recession would be difficult to come out of, with strong nations having to bail out weaker ones in order to encourage trade. Now that the United States and Europe are in a deep crisis, my thesis has been proved. In a world that is grappling for answers to the financial crisis, this book helps you understand the real causes of the financial crisis and presents likely scenarios for the future.

Learning how the lessons of an economic crisis in a small third-world country like Zimbabwe led to my accurate prediction of the global recession can improve your understanding of the principles and factors behind the crisis. This book is based on Zimbabwe's experience, which can help provide solutions for the current global recession. It has wider implications for the current global economic crisis and the new

---

1   David Chiweza, e-mail message to Bill Brown, 10 April 2000.

economic order beyond the crisis. This book's thesis emerges from the economic experiences of Zimbabwe over the past forty-five years in relation to global environmental forces. It is the synthesis of historical and current experiences under global market forces and applies lessons from these microcosmic events to explain the global economic crisis. As the saying goes, what is good for the goose is good for the gander. Zimbabwe's circumstances are akin to clinical trials on an experimental mouse whose lessons can now be applied globally.

The crisis of markets begins with the understanding that companies thrive only when their goods and services find a market. While this looks like common sense, few have seriously weighed the reasons why the United States deploys the full might of her defence and foreign policy to guard free-market policies. Markets are the foundational basis for production, and when production occurs where there is no return, entrepreneurs lose their investment. It is precisely for this reason that lenders in the financial sector find themselves sitting on non-performing loans. While the financial sector is part of a nation's investment value chain, its fortunes are tied to the success of those institutions, companies, and individuals it lends money to. It follows that a financial crisis has its origins in investment and return theory. On the basis of this understanding, the author has been able to accurately forecast the deep recession and provide fresh insight to the future direction of and solutions to the global crisis.

This book begins with an analysis of the Zimbabwean economic situation today. Zimbabwe, once referred to as Africa's jewel, has, for thirty-two years since independence in 1980, orbited in economic mediocrity, having repeatedly failed to grow her economy. To some extent the situation can be likened to the current global situation of a recession that has been variously described as deep and recurrent. Zimbabwe failed to break out into an economic growth trajectory, falling behind Singapore, Malaysia, and Kenya, countries that used to be in the same development league.

At the top of its economic problems was a declining manufacturing industry, leading to unemployment, budget deficits, and a financial and banking crisis. The consequent social problems led to the infamous land redistribution programme, leading to a political crisis and international disputes that have lasted more than a decade. The world-famous land crisis featured a black majority population, led by President Robert

Mugabe, allegedly seizing land from a small white farmer population of about four thousand. While this was seen as lawlessness, it can be likened to the aspirations of the 99 per cent movement that, as a consequence of the crisis, sees the rich 1 per cent as a target of dispossession. Once again, this brings to the fore the social implications of having a few thrive while the majority suffer.

While Zimbabwe's social and political upheavals never registered as anything more than tyranny, the world can be better enlightened to close ranks to deal with a global governance problem that can no longer be addressed in isolation. It has become clear that Zimbabwe's political crisis would not have occurred had economic conditions remained stable. Similarly, as anger rises over austerity measures in the West, Zimbabwe's case study presents lessons from a crisis that results from declining industrial performance, something that the West is now experiencing.

This book's thesis also claims that the existence of markets directly influences industrial performance. This book links Zimbabwe's economic decline to Economic Structural Adjustment Programmes dictated to it during the years 1992–1998. The major effect was that Western goods flooded domestic markets, shut down local industry, and created unemployment. This reveals the probable causes of the Western crisis: that a force similar to the one introduced into Zimbabwe has now struck the Western economies.

While a lack of markets has created internal problems for countries, *Out of the Rabble* examines the fortunes of countries that are actually enjoying rapid growth during the recession and offers explanations for the contradiction. Why are the BRICS countries thriving at a time when the world is being told there is a global crisis? If superior market forces are detrimental to domestic manufacturing, how have countries like China, India, Brazil, and South Africa surged from relative backwardness to grow their economies faster than those ranked higher on the scale of global competitiveness?

While most African countries like Zimbabwe have bent over backwards to attract investment by liberalising the financial sector, democratising the political sector, providing advanced communications infrastructure, and offering generous investment concessions, there is evidence that the secret to economic development is not based on perfect conditions. Instead, a historical study shows that nations have actually emerged from what the author calls "rabble" conditions to overtake those nations in better conditions. Why are first-world countries like the United States and Japan struggling when they rank at the top of the global competitiveness criteria? This book offers an explanation to the growth secrets of the rabble nations.

The conclusion is that these nations were able to provide five crucial factors of economic production at the same time: land, capital, labour, entrepreneurship, and markets. These critical factors, needed for economic growth, contribute a whole new dimension to economic theory. This book explains, from empirical evidence, how economic growth is made possible through these factors.

This theory stands in opposition to the universal application of the free-market doctrine. Instead, this book shows that competitively stronger nations embrace free markets, while the weaker ones must, of necessity, defend them. As weaker nations fail to defend their markets, their economic and political systems are disrupted.

With the United States and Europe facing declining industrial competitiveness and declining markets for their industries, *Out of the Rabble* raises the question of whether the West will resort to protecting markets in order to stabilise its economies. This position offers the prospect of a better and more cooperative global economic environment–an interdependent environment in which every nation state must play a role to produce for other nations or will end up playing no role in the global trade system.

This book clearly demonstrates that there was a direct correlation between stagnation in the West and economic growth for Zimbabwe, as well as the reverse–a boom in the West and a crisis in Zimbabwe. Events in Zimbabwe are a microcosm of events playing out on the global stage between Asian and Western nations, where one nation's fortunes are becoming poison for another. There are now swings in market fortunes between Western and Asian regions that defy the idea of a global crisis.

Instead, ideological and strategic challenges being presented diametrically contradict these swings in fortunes. The dominance of superior industrial power over global markets has become a threat to domestic peace. Weaker nations will demand a balance of fortunes, in which interdependency and cooperation in markets, rather than a winner-takes-all philosophy, will emerge.

As the role of markets takes centre stage, this book looks at China as a case study that reveals how a dogged governmental commitment to providing markets to its citizens has helped catapult a developing nation into an economic powerhouse. This lesson brings into focus how an underperforming Western world could be more open to negotiating markets under a new doctrine, instead of continuing the ruse of labelling China a "currency manipulator" in order to restore lost market dominance. The false strategy of espousing free-trade rhetoric on the one hand while secretly practicing protectionism on the other is a ploy that will soon be an open secret to all states, as the real threat lies in individual and unregulated responses by nations.

Out of the Rabble analyses the full range of measures China used in the "rabble conditions" that produced its current miracle. How the West and third-world countries can apply these lessons will largely depend on each country's specific conditions, but the core principles are inviolable. If the West can work harder to out-compete billions of hard-working Asians in a free-market environment, it will be able to restore its fortunes. However, such a feat presupposes that Asians are not increasing their skills and knowledge. The chances of that assumption coming true are slim; only a cooperative world will, by default, emerge.

The importance of markets in promoting industrialisation and human development dominates this book. In an age where speed of innovation and implementation is paramount, governments of slow-acting nations will have to intervene in markets on a more regular basis to guarantee market stabilisation and investment returns. The focus on providing an industrial climate necessary for economic success could unlock African industrialisation, something that has eluded the continent for a long time.

As African economies are largely service oriented, this book focuses on industrialisation through experimentation, continuous improvement, innovation, and invention, as processes that each nation can arrive at only when there are markets to consume such experimental developments. If globalisation, by offering substitutes, gives them no such chance, the challenge is whether weaker economies can acquire the knowledge and capital to get it right the first time and out-compete the technology leaders.

Faced with the handicap of a lack of technology or capital reserves large enough to beat superior competition, will they be permanently positioned to second-rate status? Globalisation means every square inch of market territory is covered–for example, with Apple and Samsung products being found in every African village. If so, how will local creativity and initiatives emerge and be sustained? How will smaller governments and countries overcome these challenges?

These are the global and national economic challenges addressed in this book.

CHAPTER 1
Concept and Methodology

OUT OF THE RABBLE is the title of this book. The thesaurus describes "rabble" as "a mob, crowd, throng, horde, swarm, gang, masses, hoi polloi, common herd, and commoners." The title therefore describes an economy that can surprise everyone by emerging out of ordinary, underrated, and deplorable circumstances. This is the example shown by the new miracle economies of China and India. Yet, in addressing this topic, I also want to convey the meaning of "rubble," as in "debris, ruins, or wreckage." That is what the emerging economies looked like just a few years ago. Indeed, their rise would not have been described as a miracle without a dramatic transformation from chaotic conditions.

Why some nations are thriving at a time that others are in crises is a matter of interest, but much more important is how a primitive-looking nation can rise to overtake those in the first world. In coming up with this understanding, I used a number of approaches.

First, as a habitual thinker, I often look for empirical evidence to support my views. Many researchers set up a hypothesis and conduct extensive research in a scientifically organised way. I do my research differently.

While I worked as a defence attaché in China from 1988 to 1992,

I developed interest in Chinese economic development. I experienced, first-hand, the economic policies of China and how they affected ordinary Chinese in a negative way. At the time I did not appreciate what they were doing, but with hindsight, what I learned was a revelation. What was of particular interest was the vast difference between their policies and my country's policies. Chinese policies stabilised the economy. Although there were various social ills, they were making astonishing progress.

The skyline of Beijing looked like a forest of construction cranes. Skyscrapers were emerging from squalor. People lived in slums along pathways that only bicycles could navigate. They were so involved in productive and creative activities that they would approach you in the street with their inventions. I got into the habit of collecting interesting innovations.

However, the quality of Chinese products was evidently poor. Who in the world could buy these products except the Chinese themselves, courtesy of an autocratic government that banned foreign products from the domestic market? The pressure for reform was gathering momentum both from within and outside. It was not a surprise that the June 4, 1989 Tiananmen Square Clashes became a watershed in Chinese economic history. On that night, more than two political forces stood opposed to each other. Rather, the force for economic change was opposing China's economic programme. The latter forces triumphed, but one wonders: What would have happened had China abandoned its programme?

The year 1992 is a significant one for my thesis. The American presidential elections were playing out. In an interview with the press, President George H. W. Bush defended his record by saying that he had done a lot for America by liberating Eastern Europe and Africa, and he urged American companies to go and conquer those markets.

This was an awakening for me. A new thesis was emerging: markets were important! That same year, after listening to the American debate and armed with the Chinese experience, I returned to find Zimbabwe in the middle of a similar debate. Which economic direction should the nation take? Our people had spent more than a decade in a Chinese-style closed economy, from 1980 to 1992. Like in China, the reform movement was gathering momentum, driven by American influence. I immediately registered that economic liberalisation would not be good for us because we were not strong enough to compete. Unlike the Chinese situation, in Zimbabwe the forces of change triumphed over gradual reforms.

Therefore, my next preoccupation was in observing the future, given my hypothesis that there would be disadvantages and that the strong would benefit. True to form, my hypothesis was confirmed over the next eight years. America, basking from African and Eastern European markets, enjoyed unprecedented growth, while little Zimbabwe allowed all of the world's best products to enter its market, destroying its industrial and creative base in the process. The nation moved from a policy of "make it" to "buy it," and as unused skills die, it lost most of its skilled labour. I was convinced of what the power of markets can do. As many groped in the dark for explanations, I felt it was time to use my understanding to predict what would happen in the future; this led to my prediction of the global crisis.

In this book, I hold out the theory that markets played a significant role in the economic fortunes of the countries under the spotlight: China and Zimbabwe. Markets similarly continue to influence the fortunes of the United States and Europe. While it is clear that markets played a dominant role in the case of China–US economic fortunes, there is uncertainty over their role in Zimbabwe during the period 1980–1990, where, in spite of a captive domestic market, industry had not grown. During this period, industry leaders actually advocated that imports fill up the market gap. If the hypothesis was going to hold out, there had to be another explanation for the stagnation. For this reason, my research expanded the hypothesis to examine all the factors of production. For production to occur, the factors of production must be deployed. But since other nations like the United States appeared to be endowed with the four factors of production, an additional factor of production must have been omitted. I therefore added "market" as a fifth factor and sought to test this against different industrial and economic development periods.

I therefore held out this template of five factors—namely, land, capital, labour, entrepreneurship, and markets—to explain the economic pitfalls and fortunes that Zimbabwe found itself in throughout its history. Whilst other researchers previously set out to classify the common things pertaining to an economic environment, I actually set out to find evidence that supported the fact that the five factors were critical ingredients to a successful economic climate, and that where one or more of the factors were missing, there would be economic challenges.

My approach is very similar to other authors, including Dan Kennedy, who wrote *Ten Million Dollar Marketing Secrets.*[2] It is similar to what Andrew Carnegie did in 1917, when the first US billionaire told a young writer, Napoleon Hill, that there were set principles for becoming wealthy and successful that could be catalogued, learned, and taught.

Carnegie had Hill interview everybody who was achieving great things in the United States in order to understand what the commonalities were. Hill called them Laws of Success, which was later written into the book *Think and Grow Rich.* Carnegie believed that the differences amongst successful individuals were unimportant. What actually mattered were the similarities of their actions and beliefs.

Tom Peters's *In Search of Excellence* essentially applied the "Think and Grow Rich" approach to companies instead of individuals. It looked at what great companies had in common. Peters listed eight common themes that dominated the business sector.

The relevance of these books to mine is the hypothesis and the framework that I use to explain a variety of economic crises. Using what I call the "industronometer," I subjected each of the countries to an analysis of five economic factors in order to determine limitations in productivity and economic progress. By raising the factors to critical success levels, I have been able to diagnose critical shortcomings of any economy at a particular time.

The science of critical success factor analysis is commonly practiced in management circles. When these five factors are applied, they explain why some countries suffer periods of economic malaise. The United States, for example, has arguably had all four of the traditional factors of production in abundance, yet without the fifth—markets—its whole system appears to have been thrown into confusion.

Through my lifelong experience and observations, I have picked out

---

2   Dan Kennedy Insider Circle, "Ten Million Dollar Marketing Secrets to Instantly Transform Any Business or Sales Career": *Unlock the Door to Your Financial Freedom*, accessed 13 March 2012, www.dankennedy. com.

a consistent set of similarities in some of the BRICS countries, including the best periods of my nation's economic history, which explain their growth (or lack of it). These similarities include the following:

- Each of the countries has had a market for the goods produced by its citizens regardless of their quality.
- Their citizens had access to the factors of production: land, capital, and labour.
- A significant majority of people were involved in productivity.
- Markets were immune to foreign competition.
- The original performance environment was deplorable but quickly changed to excellent.

During my four years in China, I was also responsible for Pakistan and North Korea. I took many shopping trips to Hong Kong, which was then a spot of civilisation in the middle of rubble. Of those four places, China, emerging from nearly half a century of self-imposed isolation, was worse off, followed by Pakistan. North Korea had its own character but certainly showed more order than China. The rest of the countries in the vicinity, such as Japan, Singapore, and Malaysia, were much more advanced.

I had the occasion to peep into India back in 1990, after landing at what used to be Bombay. Although India was already being tipped as a growing military power in the region, she was evidently backward. It was infamous for its slums and millions of poor. Just from television footage of India, the chaotic conditions were unmistakably rubble. Its cars and products could not have appealed to any international markets. For decades the industry had served its own people with mediocre products. How the automaker Tata could emerge from this backwardness to become a global company is evidence of the role played by the domestic markets to support the infant years.

Brazil was in serious economic difficulties from 1981 to 1993 in a crisis that is now referred to as "the lost decade." During this period Brazil suffered a record 30,000 per cent inflation[3], and its crisis hogged world attention. For a country that experienced so many challenges, the

---

3   Ruban Selva, "A Short History of Inflation in Brazil", accessed 14 November 2011, http://ezinearticles.com/?expert=Ruban_Selva.

temptation was to write it off, as other economies were relatively stable. I had not visited Brazil before, but as I read its history, I could see that it went through a period of isolation. Isolation becomes an important condition for explaining the concept of markets.

South Africa, which until 1994 was under crippling sanctions as a result of its apartheid policies, is another dark horse that the world never really imagined could be counted among the BRICS countries. In the fifteen-year period from 1980 to 1995, South Africa registered GDP growth from USD80 Bn to USD151 Bn, an increase of USD71 Bn. However, when we compare with the fifteen years from independence in 1994 to 2010, she choked up a whopping USD212 Bn GDP increase to USD363 Bn.[4] The economic projections for BRICS countries continue to increase, with South Africa projecting GDP of USD522 Bn in 2011. All this growth is happening in the middle of the global crisis.

There are, however, some common characteristics that set apart those nations that have now surged ahead of others even in the crisis.

1) Firstly, the isolation of domestic markets appears to have been common. China, India, South Africa, and Brazil have a history of domestic market isolation. With this isolation came market monopoly and all the growth payoffs that accrued to the people. Except for South Africa, the rest deliberately self-isolated themselves by shutting out foreign imports.

2) Secondly, because of self-reliance, they had a high proportion of citizens involved in making things. Attendant to that policy was the very absence of international production standards. The products, the housing programmes, the factories, and anything they did represented a poor local standard.

Hence, it gave that appearance of chaos, yet beneath these activities was the development and experience of a local knowledge base. This knowledge and basic skills development would become the fuel for a miracle economy. It could be said that knowledge without skills is redundant and knowledge with skills becomes explosive. This is important, as we will see that the first stage of isolation was often ignored, as people gave more value to the rapid development that became visible only at the time the economy was opened to international technological

4   "Economy of South Africa": *Historical Statistics*, accessed 2012, http://en.wikipedia.org/economy_of_South_Africa#Historical_statistics.

exchanges. However, if economic openness was the driving factor, it would have been logical for the United States and Europe to stay ahead of others that way.

A look at the background of the United States and Japan, as they rose to become world economic powers, reveals a familiar path: a period of rabble, in-house isolation in which domestic markets are protected, and a period of outsider disdain, followed by mouth-gaping economic progress. What then is the secret in the rabble, something that we often want to ignore as we, instead, look at and imitate the glitter of modernised economies?

The secret is a climate where ordinary people can be involved in creating products and be rewarded enough to reinvest in continuous improvement. This is why markets assume the most dominant position in creating these conditions. It is to be observed that these countries' economic conditions allowed Tata to grow into a global auto giant. While Proton, Malaysia's domestic car, has greater access to technology than Tata had then, it is postulated that its growth has suffered from imports that gave Malaysian domestic markets better world brands.

Countries in technology leadership positions are able to achieve a continuous improvement status for as long as they are making a profit. An examination of emerging economies of the BRICS countries reveals similarities in a pre-emergent inward-looking profile (either imposed or self-imposed), a greater degree of self-reliance, and people making their own things without too much concern about what other nations were doing. Ordinary people get involved in creative and economic activity on a wide scale. Product quality is low and the standards are mostly set by local best practice. The government seems overly tolerant and patient with the poor quality and adopts the position "good or bad, it doesn't matter," so long as they are making products in the country.

The transformation from poor quality to state of the art follows a process that was aptly described by Singaporean Researchers,[5] who coined the five stages of development (coined the "Five *I*s") when they observed the path to Japanese industrial triumph.

The process follows these stages:

---

5   Chow-Hou Wee, Khai Sheang Lee, and Bambang Walujo Hidajat, *Sun Tzu, War and Management: Application to Strategic Management and Thinking* (Addison-Wesley, 1996).

Imitation
Improvement
Improvisation
Innovation
Invention

Imitation is a period of copying other nations' products. This is the period where products are of poor and deplorable quality. They would not find markets anywhere except at home. In the process of imitation, vital learning and knowledge takes place.

This leads naturally to a stage of improvement, where each successive sale leads to a profit that is reinvested into improvement.

The third stage is improvisation, a situation where societal challenges and problems are resolved through a combination of multiple technologies that lead to useful products. For example, a wheelbarrow combines a wheel, tube extrusion, and pan-forging technologies.

The process leads to innovation, a period of improving mastery of doing things marked by notable quality improvements, localisation of identity, and originality to existing products.

Finally, the development process rises to the invention stage, where knowledge has been so fully mastered that the creative genius of the people begins to make its own discoveries.

In an environment where there is mass participation by people, the rate of development begins to take on a multiplier factor that cannot be quantified. Where the reputation of the nation's products abroad used to be deplorable, a decade or so later, the miracle begins and beautiful products start being exported from these once backward economies. Their image changes so much that we forget that they used to be in the rabble. Interestingly, in 2006, I visited the Canton Fair; it was the first time I had been to China since 1992. There I was offered several distributorships of Chinese auto companies. I did not take them because they looked just too amateurish to be bought by anyone in my country. Now, just six years down the line, I am kicking myself because there are no less than five brands that have made inroads into the South African and Zimbabwean markets, with acceptance levels growing rapidly.

It is notable that various schools have concerned themselves more with studying the metamorphosis, transformation, and outcome of an economy with little apparent interest in the conditions that prevailed while the current economies were in the "cocoon" stage. Contrary to the norms, these conditions are what I call the secrets to a miracle economy. Therefore, as we observe the miracle economies of China and India, we might want to remember that they emerged from the rabble through something that resembles chaos theory.

Chaos theory refers to an apparent lack of order in a system that nevertheless obeys particular laws or rules; this understanding of chaos is synonymous with *dynamical instability*, a condition discovered by the physicist Henri Poincaré in the early twentieth century that refers to an inherent lack of predictability in some physical systems.[6] I am saying that this rabble is a climatic condition that essentially obeyed the influence of the conventional four underlying factors of production, to which my own addition of markets completes the five critical factors to economic success.

Various countries succeed by leveraging markets in different ways. Some countries have successfully leveraged dominance in a single industry or product. Petroleum-exporting countries, mineral-rich countries, or small nations with global multinational companies can sufficiently leverage their concentrated industrial power to the benefit of its citizens. Few countries in the third world have any local brand that reaches the world markets. It is these that are most affected and disconnected from the world trading system. Balancing trade is traditionally left to economic forces and fiscal and monetary authorities, but it will increasingly take on a political involvement as market forces fail to correct the imbalance. Those nations that have risen out of the rabble did so first with political measures. Gradually their industrial competencies rose so sharply that their trade policies changed from protective to imperial free-trade stances.

This book discusses whether the West can sustain free-trade policies without falling into the fate of third-world countries.

I am convinced that the solutions to the problems in modern economies lie in distilling and replicating the rabble conditions that led to the rise of new miracle economies. If you are going to replicate

---

6   "Tech Target, The Chaos Theory", accessed March 2012, http://whatis.
    techtarget.com/definition/chaos-theory.

a plant, you must think of the seed and ground, and not focus on its mature stage. Unfortunately, as economies advance, imitators tend to forget formative stages of the growth. I have tracked this phenomenon and developed tools that can diagnose the developmental challenges of each economy. Through this analysis, I have developed a view of what the future of the world will be.

Figure 1: Prediction of Global Recession

Abel City

From: Abel City <hitncity@africaonline.co.zw>
To: Bill Brown <
Sent: Monday, April 10, 2000 9.58 PM
Subject: ZIMBABWE SITUATION - MY PERSPECTIVE (PERSONAL)

Zimbabwe's present circumstances emanate from its past and the history of colonialism that dates back 1890s when the first white settlers settled in Zimbabwe

Structural adjustment programmes have hurt our economies here. My prediction is that they are going to hurt their sponsors more in the near future. You need only look at the fact that now we can not trade with the world any more, and someone in South Africa is hurting because we cannot buy from him. Soon that someone will not be able to buy from America and someone in America will lose a job or a company may close down. The second recession will hurt the rich nations badly and will be difficult to come out of. Globalization represents the last move of territorial expansion of markets. Any future growth of markets will have to be a qualitative one. However this qualitative growth cannot take place when western nations are pursuing policies that kill third world growth. Its like the cow that kills the grass it feeds on.

If the above were to happen (which is very likely) the western world will have to be socially adjusted the concept of sharing along socialist lines. This being an ideology to which the are sworn enemies will mean they will try to force open markets to keep traditional percentage growth mentality. What I see is that the South and the North have their interests clashing already even before the conflicts have begun. This is because if Africans cannot win in foreign markets then they must at least win at home. Globalization is giving them no such chance. If they are to remain peaceful, they may have to succumb and let their economies go down and wait for the goat to die before the grass can spring again. If they have to keep growing present economies they have to be protected from predators while the watering takes place. The world must realize that it needs wealthy nations to trade with or else they may have to give us their money to buy their goods. Have you tried see-saw with a kid? You do all the jumping while it does nothing. Such is the economic imbalance being created. At the end the world will be equal. There is more on this topic than I can possibly say on this mail.

Well there you are BB. Just what an African like me thinks about this. Things are getting ugly and my guess is that there will be some scuffles. Much of what will surface are issues of corruption and self interest and the real issues are a struggle for racial supremacy on the land of the Africans.

DAVID CHIWEZA

CHAPTER 2

Zimbabwe's Economic Situation Today

In 2009, Zimbabwe's ten-year political and economic crisis culminated in a Global Political Agreement, agreed to after bitterly contested elections in 2008. With a peace dividend, Zimbabwe's optimism was high and the media reported increased confidence in the country's economy. For some time, politicians also rode a wave of optimism, with nobody warning of the potentially calamitous economic conditions creeping into the country. Three years down the road, that optimism has been eroded as companies and individuals face rapidly deteriorating and stressful economic conditions.

The poor performance results of listed companies indicate that the economy is in trouble. Media reports show that many companies are not only in serious debt, they also are struggling to raise much-needed capital. There are many negatives on the manufacturing sector: local capital markets are virtually dry, and banks are laden with doubtful or non-performing loans.

The financial sector is in trouble. The illusion of hope has faded after the initial banking ratios of non-performing loans were revised from 9 to 90 per cent. That means the banks are technically insolvent. Government has mooted the idea to create a fund to take over all the banks' bad debts. Just like Western banking bailouts, will this solution suffice without arresting the cause of it?

Capacity utilisation hardly exceeds 50 per cent. Companies are finding it difficult to regain market share. Plants and machinery are aged. The city of Bulawayo turned into a ghost town as close to ninety companies closed down in the year 2011 alone.[7] Of those still employed, many are going without pay. Retrenchments are the order of the times in a country with up to 80 per cent unemployment.

Infrastructure remains very much in decay and there is a general debt crisis, even at personal level, with money supply constraints running deep. The global financial crisis is evident in Zimbabwe, as heavily indebted companies threaten to sink the banking sector. The knock-on effects could result in unimaginable consequences for the entire economy.

Government itself is threatened with a shutdown, with revenue targets being revised downwards. The clamour for civil service pay increases has been put on hold as government fails to meet salary requirements. This is happening at a time when all the floodgates of liberalisation and investment attraction remain open and every effort to market the country is being made. At a time when even the West itself is in dire need for jobs, will this pay off? The answer lies in the discussions that follow.

Let us put the country's economic situation in its proper perspective. Zimbabwe moved away from hyperinflation through the dollarisation of the economy on 12 February 2009. There was apparent nominal growth in real terms, accompanied by some outward signs of green shoots, as in early spring, but it should not have masked reality. What was being referred to as "growth" was deceptive self-aggrandisement, much more driven by the desire for political favour ahead of elections than realism. Media reports that Zimbabwe led Africa in annual economic growth rates were misleading, as they came on the back of a false economic trajectory.

---

7   "Godfrey Marawanyika, IOL Mobile", 29 May 2012, accessed 15 July 2012, http://m.iol.co.za/article/views/s/9/a/68706.

While the 9.3 per cent economic growth rate[8] touted made for a good political campaign, the results have not and will not be felt by ordinary citizens in the foreseeable future. The term "economic growth," which is an "increase in a country's productive capacity, as measured by comparing gross national product (GNP) in a year with the GNP in the previous year,"[9] conceals an important marker, which is the peak economic level Zimbabwe previously achieved.

Given that GNP fell over the past decade, a more appropriate understanding of what happened is an economic recovery. An economic recovery is a phase in an economic cycle where employment and output begins to rise to their normal levels after a recession or slump.[10] The reality in Zimbabwe is that we are still seeing 50 per cent and below industrial capacity utilisation. This hardly describes a situation where industry has returned to its normal levels. Therefore, it is not growth at all, but a "recovery" from a hole that the economy sank into in the last decade (2000–2010). Growth can only be realised when new companies are set up and when established production and revenue records are surpassed. In practice, the typical Zimbabwean recovery measures are based on the injection of working capital into existing capacity with little or no fresh investment in plant and machinery.

Because Zimbabwe has not learned from her past, she has deceived herself and wasted much more valuable time by seeing this recovery as economic growth. Recovery is easy, because the productive assets are already in place, even though we are struggling to regain market share. The real test is when we have to push upward from the normal level of capacity utilisation and economic activity. Can the current growth rates under "recovery" circumstances be sustained after normalisation, or will we settle into another decade of economic stagnation?

Unless our new economic policies demonstrate a capacity to sustain

---

8   Bulawayo24.com, "Zimbabwe's Economic Growth Could Exceed Forecast", accessed April 2012, http://www.bulawayo24.com/index-idbusiness-sc-economy-byo-4458-article-Zimbabwe+economic+growth+could+exceed+forecast%3A+Biti.html.

9   Businessdictionary.com, "Economic Growth", accessed May 2012, http://www.businessdictionary.com/definition/economic-growth.html#ixzz1pZUioEek

10   Businessdictionary.com, "Recovery", accessed May 2012, http://www.businessdictionary.com/defi nition/recovery.html#ixzz1pZT8GW3c.

new investments and markets at the projected levels, this optimism may be misplaced. Since the country slid into negative growth a long time ago and is still in sub-zero economic growth, there can be no talk of growth until it moves past the zero mark. The manufacturing sector, a credible indicator of productivity, is still in its doldrums as evidenced by nearly 80 per cent shelf space in supermarkets occupied by foreign products. This means domestic companies have not yet attained their pre-dollarisation production levels.

The threat to Zimbabwe is the risk of another misdiagnosis of the economy, which will, in turn, yield defective economic strategies. There is a need to rethink and match political rhetoric to reality. In 1992, Zimbabweans had the opportunity to make economic choices about the future of their country. They clearly made the wrong choices by choosing Economic Structural Adjustment Programme (ESAP) policies. Twenty years later, there is a growing consensus that it was wrong, but ironically, despite this consensus and apparent condemnation, the structures remain in place. There is evidently a drought of options to take. Therefore, why expect different results if we keep doing the same things?

In the last five years Zimbabwe has pushed empowerment programmes where local people have been allowed to take ownership of at least 51 per cent of local companies, and yet no change has occurred. While this empowerment has the effect of localising the companies, the companies themselves remain subordinate to market forces imposed upon them by globalisation, in the process, destroying the market factor in the economy.

Zimbabweans are perennial optimists, always looking forward with hope, and yet, sadly, it has always been a tale of deferred hope–we are forever chasing, as does one trying to catch up with the horizon. When will they arrive? I believe they have to do things differently if they are ever to reach their destination.

In the next chapter, I describe the origin of Zimbabwe's economic problems and their relation to global and regional factors.

CHAPTER 3

Zimbabwe's Economic Problems and Their Connection to Regional and Global Economic Factors

ZIMBABWE'S PROBLEMS ARE A microcosm of the wider global economic challenges faced today. She has lived the full circle of economic challenges and experiences for the world. In the last decade, from 2000 to date, Zimbabweans have seen crippling economic challenges–shortages in fuel, food, basic commodities, and cash; high unemployment; and a soaring rate of inflation. The Zimbabwe dollar became the least valued currency unit in history, undergoing three re-denominations, with a final high face-value paper denomination of a $100 trillion banknote[11] (10^{14}). Such was the scale of economic and social hardships. In 2009 the country scrapped its currency, choosing instead to trade in foreign currency only.

This has given rise to a liquidity crisis as people find it difficult to trade. The whole country has to depend on foreign currency inflows

---

11   *Wikipedia*, "Zimbabwe Dollar," accessed April 2012, http://en.wikipedia.org/wiki/Zimbabwean_dollar.

in order to exchange goods. This is itself stunting growth. The balance of trade is against the country where the country's imports exceeded $8.6 Bn against the exports of $3.5 Bn. This represents a net foreign currency outflow of $5 Bn.[12] How the country can finance domestic trade is really anybody's guess. On paper, there should be no money for domestic trade, as imports cancel out exports. The better explanation is that this is financed from remittances from abroad and borrowings.

Yet in its microcosmic nature, Zimbabwe's economic challenges mirror the current global crisis facing the United States and EU. These countries each began from a dominant economic position in their regions, and then they suffered the loss of competitive advantage and markets that plunged them into an economic crisis marked by social and political unrest. A new and dominant industrial power has displaced them. It is basically the principle of substitution that is at play.

Will the United States and EU come out of the crisis by applying more of the policies that have worked before? Zimbabwe, for instance, continued on the same path of economic liberalisation without success. It has watched the trade deficit grow while it put its faith in free markets. It has had a more ready excuse in the smart sanctions imposed by the United States and European governments. It is highly unlikely that the United States and EU will succeed by pursuing more free-trade strategies. Like Zimbabwe, they will fail because of the dynamism of their competitors.

Zimbabwe was a dominant regional economic power before South Africa's entry into the Southern African Development Community (SADC) in 1994. Until that time, Zimbabwe was a major source of imports for the region, with a thriving industrial base that held much promise for the future. Two major events altered the balance of industrial power.

First, in 1992, there was the misguided diagnosis that the country needed to adopt Economic Structural Adjustment Programmes (ESAP). The programme came with, among other things, the need to open markets, liberalise financial markets, privatise government companies, relinquish government control, and allow market forces to play their part. The benefits, it was envisaged, would accrue through increased

---

12   Zimstats, "Summary", accessed August 2012, http://www.zimstat. co.zw/dmdocuments/Trade/Bulletin/Summary.pdf.

investment attraction, increased creativity, improved efficiency, and a successful economy.

To understand ESAP better, we need to understand how the economy functioned before then. First of all, the regulated Rhodesian/Zimbabwean economy had been designed to function as a system. It emphasised strong government control and management of the economic system. The system revolved around a domestic-driven economy with local production of food, goods, and services. What was not locally produced would be imported, and what was surplus to local consumption was exported. Its primary focus was a national service mentality, with export and import functions designed to be by-products of excesses and shortfalls. Commerce existed for the sole purpose of distributing goods and services to the people as partners with local industry.

An economic system, like any system, is an organised, purposeful structure regarded as a whole and consisting of interrelated and interdependent elements (components, entities, factors, members, parts, etc.). These elements continually influence one another (directly or indirectly) to maintain their activity and the existence of the system, in order to achieve the goal of the system.[13]

As an eco-system, it has to be self-existing (i.e., even immune to external forces). Government regulation plays a central role to ensure fair play in markets, avoiding duplication in investment and overpricing. The structure in Zimbabwe was so well considered and regulated that it gave rise to a corporate state, where all institutions were intricately related in a coordinated manner.

For example, as part of a system, commerce could not work against industry. Instead, it supported local industry instead of harming it. In contrast, in Zimbabwe today, it does not matter how well agriculture performs. The selfish and reckless commerce still imports produce in pursuit of profit objectives rather than to provide markets for industry. Commerce has abandoned its primary distributive function, where it ought to distribute local products and provide for shortfalls or sell off surpluses. To that extent, the Zimbabwean government had knowledge of what was happening in industry, and it planned and authorised levels

---

13 Businessdirectory.com, "System", accessed March 2012, http://www. businessdictionary.com/definition/system.html.

of imports. It even controlled and allocated foreign currency. This enabled the government to balance trade and build foreign currency reserves, which in turn stabilised the economy.

The destruction of that economic system in favour of individualism spelt doom for the country's economy. ESAP ensured there would be no central control and made it difficult for the government to direct a corporate strategy. It is like trying to drive a stripped car. Whilst the components are all present, they need to be bolted up together for the car to be driveable. The notion and perception of strong leadership as dictatorship and the elevation of consumerism above strategic sense made this situation worse. It is now very difficult to discern what Zimbabwe's economic system is. Instead of an economic system where every part gives and receives, there are many organisations operating like parasites, taking from the system and not adding value to it.

A number of systems challenges have emerged in the process. For example, a company importing products to compete with its own industry ceases to serve the system but pursues only profits; similarly, the retailer disarms and cripples industry by bypassing the supply chain through the import of competing products. These actions block the flow of wealth through the entire system. Unfortunately, industries in many weak countries either are not integrated or have no capacity to be integrated into the world supply chain, to the extent that they cannot give or take from the system.

Liberalisation in Zimbabwe brought about systems chaos. In contradiction with systems theory, economic decisions with systemswide implications were decentralised to individuals and the economic system was paralysed. Companies and individuals now make market choices. There are no more corporate state goals, and where they are present, fiscal policy measures have had little influence on individual choices, making it difficult to direct state strategies. There is an appearance of state control, and yet actions are independent of state control. Therefore, the state is stuck with a trade deficit that it is too weak to correct. Its own state organs are working against each other. The Ministry of Industry wants to promote local industry, but the Commerce and Trade arm is promoting regional and international market integration at a time when its industry is unable to compete. With liberalisation, entry barriers have been lowered and cash rich foreigners buy up Zimbabwe's lucrative assets cheaply.

In recent years, the government has tended to trim social services in favour of privatisation, thinking it would be less expensive to do so. That has not worked, leading to deteriorating service delivery. Zimbabwe's once vibrant health and education services have suffered as a result, with government being forced to abandon free education and health programmes. The welfare state system is gone, leaving citizens who have neither jobs nor access to welfare to vent their anger on the government itself.

After all the euphoria of liberalisation, it was not surprising that the results were quite to the contrary. The influx of foreign goods on the market closed local industries, stiffened competition, and made investment in small markets like Zimbabwe's quite unattractive. The sophisticated communications infrastructure, serving only to facilitate import trade, meant foreign corporations became more interested in selling than investing. Informal businesses increased at the expense of formal businesses, and as a result the tax base shrank, leading to the destruction of service delivery.

The second major event was the admission of South Africa into the Southern African Development Community at the end of apartheid in 1994. South Africa had two distinct advantages over Zimbabwe that helped displace it as the dominant economic power in the region. She had an industrial manufacturing base superior to Zimbabwe's and was more attractive as an investment destination with the most advanced facilities and service delivery in the region. The unveiling of South Africa as an import source for other African countries simply overshadowed Zimbabwe in all attractions. But worse still, Zimbabwe had no control over its citizens' choices. Zimbabwe immediately started to suffer an internal meltdown, as she not only imported from South Africa, but her regional export markets also switched to that nation.

Apart from South Africa's advanced manufacturing, buoyed by a skilled white workforce of six million, she had sophisticated port and airport facilities that made it the centre of all communications in the African hinterland. She became a port of choice for most international companies, many of which set up bases there. South Africa, therefore, became not only a source of manufactured products, but a conduit for re-export and transit business for all international exports into Africa. As a result, most international companies have distribution agreements with South African companies. African countries in the interior have to pay a premium for South African handling. Like Hong Kong was to China, South Africa has profited from being a "bridgehead" into inland Africa. This of course has given her enormous growth prospects that have outweighed the effects of globalisation on her home markets and industry. However, even with these advantages, South Africa is increasingly feeling the pressure of globalised markets, particularly in as far as it has affected its unprotected textile and poultry sector.

As South Africa has affected Zimbabwe, the emergence of China, India, and other BRICS countries on the world economic scene have apparently created the same economic challenges for the United States and EU countries. The Chinese and Indian models of development threaten the traditional economic dominance of the Western powers.

China, for example, has grown in multiple technologies. They have expertise in almost all products of the world, thereby giving other countries no market niche to compete. Unlike Germany, which is strongest in automobiles and machine tools, or the United States, which is strongest in high technology, design, and entertainment, or the United Kingdom, whose strength is in financial services, the Asian industrial power is advancing like a swarm of locusts, licking up everything green, from the treetops to the grass on the ground. Such an approach is resulting in the gradual displacement of the United States and EU countries from global markets, and for the first time they are feeling the effects of something that they have not anticipated. In this way, they are duplicating the experience of third-world countries like Zimbabwe.

Indeed, what is good for the goose is good for the gander. What affected little Zimbabwe from a subregional point of view may well be the same forces affecting the United States and Europe today. These are principles with universal application. Therefore, the reverse is also true: what will work for Zimbabwe will also work for the large economies of the world. Whether you live in Africa, the Americas, Asia, or Europe, globalisation forces will unite world opinion around the collective desire for survival.

The lessons from little Zimbabwe will be pivotal to understanding this emerging new world order.

CHAPTER 4

Globalisation and Its Impact on Zimbabwe

To THRIVE ECONOMICALLY IN the age of globalisation, a country first needs to position itself in a strategic fit with global forces, trends, and currents. This is not supposed to be merely copying or imitating, but rather taking advantage of or exploiting these forces to advantage. Just as you would lay your traditional fish trap in the narrow flowing part of a river to catch fish, we must correctly interpret globalisation in order to position ourselves for success. This sounds obvious, but its economic contextual interpretation is what informs this thesis. The emphasis is on positioning itself, because African countries are usually positioned by others seeking economic advantage through visions and strategies contrary to theirs, or through ill-considered imitations of other nations acting from their own economic conditions.

For example, the Economic Structural Adjustment Programme (ESAP) was a vision and strategy that benefited Western industrial powers, while the current push towards regional economic integration is best suited to benefit South Africa's superior industry. As a matter of principle, each country must relate to the global forces in accordance with its unique and concrete conditions. It must, therefore, be recognised that failure to appreciate the direction of the global forces will inevitably make us fail to position ourselves for economic advantage.

In a rapidly changing world, foresight has become very important. Long range plans often become obsolete in a matter of months. The information age has accelerated the speed of change to such a degree that there is often a gap between the speed of conceptualisation and the speed of implementation. As a result, obsolescence is happening faster now than before. At the rate Apple is churning out its product upgrades, many consumers wonder which product to buy and how long they can keep it before it becomes outdated. The real risk to a company that is trying to enter the technology race is that it may position itself at an entry technology level, but even before it sets up its plant, the technology has moved on. Therefore, predicting the future with a fair amount of accuracy may save us the costly pain of false starts and outdated plans.

Will weaker nations cope with the pace of change, or will governments hold off change? It is precisely this phenomenon that has cost Zimbabwe several generations of underdevelopment. It is not that Zimbabweans cannot dream but that their dreams never see the light of day. However, because of lack of foresight, there is fear that even at this late hour, Zimbabwe is poised to make another costly misjudgement.

Globalisation of markets appeared at the end of the long recession of 1979–1992. It coincided with democratisation of African and Eastern European countries. It also coincided with trade liberalisation across the globe and an economic boom for the United States. This market globalisation led Zimbabwe and many other smaller countries to abandon the principles of self-reliance and import substitution. Companies with global reach used globalisation of markets to serve their rapidly increasing industrial output. As output increased, local markets in many nations could no longer absorb all products, which led to recessions, production cutbacks, and the closure of many Western companies.

Something of historical importance has happened here, and many may miss it. It led to my prediction of the current deep recession. For more than a decade from 1979 to 1992, US industrial capacity seemed contained in a holding place, like water in a dam. And when a dam is full, there is nowhere else the water can go. But then, in the late '80s, with democratisation and free-trade policies, in what was referred to as "the breaking of the iron curtain," the walls were broken. The water suddenly found new territories, signifying the US economic boom of the '90s. But then the boom hit the next wall, in the form of market territories that could no longer be expanded. This last wall, as I envisioned, would be difficult to breach.

Having come out of the 1979 recession, through the breach of the iron curtain, this recession provides no new walls to breach, an indication that market territories will always reach their limits. If so, where will the next wave of growth come from?

I realised that the global powers, to sustain their growth, would need wealthier nations to trade with. But if so, how would weaker nations emerge from the crippling dominance of market forces without protectionism? How would they avoid becoming de facto colonies of the larger powers? How would smaller nations achieve political integration, to compensate the vanquished with welfare support?

Even as early as 2000, it became apparent that a new and deep global recession would occur. For trade to continue, there would have to be major reforms in international trade, or else a world government should emerge, one that would bail out or redistribute wealth to those nations that could not rise.

I realised that international trade had lost its two-dimensional growth approach. It was left with only one dimension. The first dimension was based on the lateral direction of territorial expansion, while the second dimension is based on an increase in the buying power of nations (i.e., either with prices coming down or with incomes going up). However, we now realise that globalisation has contained territorial expansion. There will be no new territories; rather, only new qualitative markets will emerge, and here is where hope and opportunity lies for the world.

We might want to pause here and ask the question, "Was globalisation of markets wrong?"

It is important to note that, at its inception, intellectual discourse was deeply divided on the merits of globalisation and free trade. It would appear to me that it was always right for those nations that had stronger economies to pursue globalisation. In fact, territorial expansion of markets has been a consistent thread of truth throughout history. Trade has always been on the march, from the village to the global level. It is actually the fulfillment of destiny.

What has become a puzzle, though, is the discontinuity of globalisation. What is next in this thread? With no more new markets to discover, the stage for fierce competition has started. In the past, in battles for pasture, relief was always found by becoming nomadic. That is no longer an option. Globalisation has put that in check and is rewriting the rules. But what better opportunity do we have for a new economic order, as when the global economic superpowers find themselves in that position of need? And, in that debate, the voices of small countries like Zimbabwe have to be heard.

On the other hand, globalisation of markets was always directional, being pushed from the stronger to the weaker economies. First, it did not make sense that countries invited their own competition, and second, it was always going to be difficult to build competencies without a secure home turf to practice. The Zimbabwean domestic debate is at a transitional point, where there is stark evidence of the folly of adopting globalisation and its free-trade concepts. The evidence is crystal clear: pro-free-market concept forces were wrong or, at best, deceptive.

Globalisation and free-market concepts failed on account of divided interests. There are clearly few winners in an open competition. Unfortunately, this is a competition of survival, and when a nation has lost, it must find compensation for that loss somewhere. A success for one country is a loss for another. Blame has to fall somewhere. While free markets are a good concept and certainly promote creativity, they can do much damage in a global environment that takes no responsibility for the vanquished.

In America, for example, and many other countries, free markets have worked under the "common market-common political borders" principle. That principle applies to compensation for loss. Within the same state, one market loss translates to a gain within the same political system. The state is able to spread the gains and losses to all citizens, thereby creating harmony.

Within globalisation, we have seen how the system plays out, with US bailouts of companies and EU bailouts of member states. It may be said that despite German complaints at having to bail out other nations, it was her industrial power that swallowed the markets of the weaker nations, as the Germans turned them into bigger markets for their superior industries. Now it is the Germans' turn to give back what they took.

The principle, however, does not apply to third-world countries; they have to carry the costs of globalisation alone. South Africa will certainly not bail out Zimbabwe, rendering the principle of "common markets–uncommon political borders" unworkable. Nations will resort to self-defence by opting out of the regional trade agreements that have merely turned them into fish ponds for the stronger economies.

Let us take a moment to revisit a few key historical events to demonstrate the power of markets in industrialisation. Firstly, the acceptance of the Western market ploy (the idea that open markets were universally beneficial) was absurd because business schools never taught a company (or a country) to invite its own competition. Instead, successful companies build barriers to stifle competition and keep markets to themselves.

Microsoft, for example, cornered the markets by allegedly abusing monopoly power on Intel-based personal computers through its handling of operating system and web browser sales, where it bundled its flagship Internet Explorer web browser software with its Microsoft Windows operating system. This strategy is alleged to have been responsible for Microsoft's victory in the browser wars, as every Windows user had a copy of Internet Explorer.[14] Microsoft was smart enough to corner the market, which led to rapid growth.

What operates at the company level also operates at the national level. The rules of monopoly apply in both cases. That we were deceived into believing that open markets would lead to economic growth is now a fact of history. The economic ruins are there as evidence. Zimbabwe's clothing industry, which once was ranked superior to South Africa's, is practically dead. Zimbabwe's engineering and auto industries had become so advanced that at one point they were providing 60 per cent of local content. Not anymore. The Zimbabwe Iron and Steel Company's fortunes also died with the decline in manufacturing industries. Trinity Engineering Company used to manufacture truck bodies, while AVM and Deven Engineering built buses that were exported throughout the region. All this was made possible by the policy of local manufacturing, and in turn this supported thousands of other companies that fed into the system. Yet, when Zimbabwe resorted to importing autos and buses,

---

14 *Wikipedia*, *"United States versus Microsoft,"* accessed March 2012, http://en.wikipedia.org/wiki/United_States_v._Microsoft.

as opposed to engines and chassis only, the nation's demand for steel plummeted, and these industries were destroyed.

Zimbabwe could take a trip down memory lane and remember its radio, sound, and television industry, which was, by comparison, ahead of China's in 1988. But instead of upgrading and modernising this industry, manufacturers opened their markets to Japanese electronics so quickly that they were turned into distributors and dealers in Japanese brands. This represented a massive transfer in wealth, jobs, and the "people happiness" factor. The result was the emergence of political in-fighting that made world headlines.

In reality, the principle is that when your industry is strong, you want others to open their markets to you. When your industry is weak, it makes business sense to protect your own markets by restricting imports. These offensive and defensive strategies apply in all spheres of life. Basic economic principles suggest that supply follows demand and productivity follows markets, and yet this principle, widely applied at the business level, was violated at national levels.

For example, between 2009 and 2011, Zimbabwe's Ministry of Finance and Economic Planning irrationally insisted that companies first increase capacity utilisation before it would reintroduce tariffs on imported basic goods. What it was saying was, "Produce without a market, and then I will give you a market" (hopefully before you go bankrupt).

The consequences of this misguided policy are clear. The death of industry in the city of Bulawayo is testimony to the calamitous consequences of misjudgement, with ninety companies reportedly closing down in 2011 alone. To offer further proof of the hypothesis that markets drive economies, let us examine the historical relationships between markets and industrialisation at the national level. In Zimbabwe, there are two economic eras that help illustrate my point.

The First Era: 1979–1991

These are the years of industrial decline in the United States, on one hand, and Zimbabwean economic stagnation on the other. This era is infamous for the term "recurrent recession," which was the catchphrase that referred to the US recession. The term "recurrent" implied that the recession was stubborn; although there were massive efforts to grow the economy, the recession returned year after year. Ironically, the West is now in a new recession, known simply as a "financial crisis" and variously described as "deep" and "the recession that keeps coming back."

For the United States, the collapse of Eastern Europe and the liberalisation of African economies was a culmination of years of CIA conspiracy under the Reagan and Bush administrations. During that time, the cold war was understood to be an ideological struggle in which noble principles of democracy and freedom were advocated. With hindsight, it is now clear that a covert strategy to open markets to serve the US industrial interests was at play. The country's need for new markets to come out of the recurrent recession was the primary motivation. The United States had exhausted all internal macroeconomic and microeconomic measures without success.

Is it not a contradiction that the most advanced nation on earth, with banks awash with money, entrepreneurs with best training, and the world leader in technology could not get out of recession despite having access to quality factors of production? It had failed to jump-start the economy with federal funding of infrastructural development projects. America and her corporations had applied all her business wizardry, but the fact remained: the recession would not go away.

In Zimbabwe, the terms "economic stagnation" and "domestic economy" dominated the debate at the time. During this decade, Zimbabwe lived strictly under a very highly regulated economy inherited from the Rhodesian regime. Prior to independence in 1980, this economy had been growing, successfully enduring five years of a brutal bush war and fifteen years of British-imposed sanctions. That it had failed to grow under the new black majority rule was evident, but the diagnosis was to be flawed. While the US recession was a result of limited markets, Zimbabwe's economic problems were due to entirely different reasons.

In the period 1980–1992, Zimbabwe controlled her markets; preference was given to local manufacturing companies. Where there was no manufacturing capability, or where production capacity was inadequate, importers were given import quotas to fill up the supply gap. This enabled local industry to always retain the capacity to grow. In principle, given this captive market, economic growth should have taken place during the years 1980–1992. But other factors of production came into play, as will be more fully discussed. What is important to note, however, is that Zimbabwe had experienced relative economic stability. The quality of life of Zimbabweans increased greatly through massive investment in social services. It is in this period that Zimbabwe recorded her famed growth in education and health.

The Second Era: 1992–2000

This period was marked by the longest and biggest economic boom in the United States and a decade-long industrial and political decline for Zimbabwe. The pro-democracy reform movement had swept successfully through Eastern Europe. African democratisation rapidly took place, and the liberation of markets was completed. In the United States, *Time* magazine and *Newsweek* had many superlatives to describe the economy and Allan Greenspan. It was recorded as the biggest and longest economic boom since the 1960s. It brought a political dividend for Bill Clinton, who reportedly could not believe his good fortune.

At the same time, and just as suddenly, the tables turned in Zimbabwe. The country's economic fortunes went into a tailspin. Many companies closed, jobs were lost, the currency lost value, accusations of corruption and mismanagement were levelled against the government, and the political opposition gathered momentum. Citizens became restless and discontented. Like Americans in the former recession days, they wanted to change their government. They felt that their dream had been lost.

However, this period did not pan out like a horror movie. It had much promise and excitement for politicians and citizens. Due to liberalisation, the supply response was swift. Within three months, the country was awash with foreign products, ranging from consumer products, information technology, groceries, and drinks of all kinds. Imported luxury cars came into the economy, and at some point Zimbabwe rivalled Western countries in the number of Mercedes-Benz cars per capita, as they became standard package for executive positions.

New wholesale distribution companies were set up as conduits for foreign goods. Companies such as Jaggers Wholesalers and Makro of South Africa moved in and were stocked to the brim with foreign luxury goods. Consumers flocked there, and their management became so scornful of local products that local industry was pushed aside, being told to match the competition or close shop. The imported goods were of such a higher quality and at a lower price that local Zimbabwean companies could not compete.

Further investment came in through South African fast food franchises. In came brands like Pizza Inn, Kentucky Fried Chicken, Nando's, Creamy Inn, and others. From a citizen's point of view, consumerism looked good. The life looked brighter and offered so much choice. A number of new modern buildings sprang up, giving consumers exciting hangouts and luxury office blocks.

To a careful observer, however, all this economic success was dangerously hollow. Substitution was happening so fast that the end game was just a matter of time. Manufacturing companies were closing fast. Shelf space was being filled to near 100 per cent with foreign luxury goods, and imported food products were reaching 50 per cent. For a country that had been almost self-sufficient a decade ago, this was unbelievable and highly destructive.

Machinery and machine tools trade companies moved from trade in brand new machines to trading in used machines, as the engineering companies closed. Eventually all the companies closed, and to date there is no machinery trading company in Zimbabwe. The country moved from self-sufficiency to dependency.

On the social front, this misguided arrogance followed a now familiar pattern. The weak felt the pain first. The privileged rich were arrogant and ignored the signs. Eventually the crisis struck home, and the movement for change gathered steam, but the rich felt the heat last.

In Zimbabwe, it started with workers losing jobs, demonstrations, intermittent food riots, and disgruntled war veterans crying out for social relief. The public had no sympathy for the war veterans. They actually ridiculed them as they fought running battles with the government, to the extent of besieging the state house. Led by Chenjerai Hunzvi, they eventually forced government to pay each of the eighty thousand veterans a compensation of $50,000. Following this sudden pay-out, the Zimbabwe currency lost value by nearly 50 per cent in what was described as the "Dark Night" in Zimbabwe's history.

Instead of treating this event as a warning, the blame was pointed at war veterans for having caused the economic currency plunge and meltdown that followed. It triggered more disgruntlement, and with a looming election, calls for the change of government were getting louder. Meanwhile, it became evident that the economy was doing badly. The government of President Mugabe had nothing to show the people and was increasingly under pressure to deliver on land redistribution promises. Since 1980, there had been token land redistributions funded by Britain under the "willing buyer, willing seller" programme. When British funds ran out, intergovernment negotiations for more funding continued without yielding results. With the government fearing that it would lose elections, it was resolved that the constitution be changed to enable it to compulsorily acquire land.

Therefore, a constitutional reforms programme was initiated, and for the first time, the whites who had been politically docile mobilised in full force to defeat the new constitution in a referendum. When the no vote was passed against the new constitution, it was clear the opposition movement had gathered momentum. On the other hand, the government of President Mugabe, which was losing urban popularity, still had the rural people as allies. All they had ever wanted was land and not urban luxuries. Land became a battleground of convenience; that is, a necessity for the people and a survival option for the political party.

It therefore came as no surprise that when the people of Svosve took the initiative to invade white farms in Mashonaland East, the government was disarmed and adopted an "I told you so" attitude. When the government was called to forcibly remove the invaders, it stood by them and the movement soon spread. Government then rode on the wind of people-initiated movement and worked with them to bring sanity through a controversial fast track land redistribution programme. In reality, government had no choice but to do the fast track programme to fulfil the aspirations of its key constituency.

From 2000 to 2008, the land battle played out, and the British and US governments were brought in to intervene. Some lives were lost in the process. US, British, and EU sanctions were imposed against Zimbabwe. Further rounds of civil strife ensued as the Morgan Tsvangirai-led Movement for Democratic Change rode on the urban discontent and became a front for the anti-Mugabe alliance.

A few key principles are worthy of note here. When a lake dries out, it starts at the shallow end. While the destruction was happening, the privileged continued to ignore the economic indicators and always found scapegoats. Eventually, when trouble knocked at home, when their value was being destroyed, action was precipitated.

The same thing is happening in Europe. First it was Portugal, Spain, Greece, and Italy, and now Hungary and Britain. There are indications that France could follow suit. Do we really need to endure the full pain before we can embrace managed change? Will Europe wait for Germany to suffer first before the message hits home?

Secondly, few people are taking the foundations of the Zimbabwean meltdown into consideration. While there are many events that brought Zimbabwe to her current position, memory is short and there is a risk in carrying out a superfluous analysis. The correction need not be based on the final events that caused the problem. It has to be based on the foundations of the matter.

In this case, the foundation is really the crisis of markets. Any solution that does not address competitiveness and markets is bound to fail, whether in Zimbabwe or the world at large.

CHAPTER 5

The Bush Administration's Strategy for World Markets

FROM 1989 ONWARDS, WITH the Soviet Union and its Communist doctrine largely discredited, it was easier to push for capitalist market liberalisation as an alternative. The Bush administration was clear about the value of markets to the United States. It was also clear that it was set to take the markets from others in those territories. These were covert objectives that could only be gleaned from the activities and policies pursued.

With pro-democracy movements sweeping across Eastern Europe, democracy and trade liberalisation policies were pushed through using the stick-and-carrot method. A country had to liberalise its economy in order to receive foreign direct investments. Leaders of countries that liberalised their economies were showered with praise, often invited to Western capitals, and received international awards and favourable media endorsement. Meanwhile, those that did not comply faced shrinking foreign direct investment, aid, and access to World Bank and IMF loans. The United States actively engaged in funding and sponsoring "US-friendly" opposition political movements and hordes of non-governmental organisations.

With the advent of a global media, these values became so popularised that few governments could stand against the "winds of change." In southern Africa, for example, Mozambique, Zambia, Zimbabwe, Angola, Namibia, and Tanzania were each pursuing policies of self-reliance that were contrary to US policy objectives. The United States viewed the leaders of these countries, who had led their people through wars of liberation, as radicals stuck in Soviet-era ideology. The United States needed moderates who would advance their interests. In Mozambique, Samora Machel was killed in a mysterious plane crash after he had been opposed by the South African and Western-sponsored Mozambique National Resistance Movement. His successor, Foreign Minister Joachim Chissano, adopted moderate policies that accommodated Western interests and were widely hailed and accepted by Western press. In Zambia, Kenneth Kaunda faced a popularised pro-democracy Fredrick Chiluba, who led the Movement for Multi-Party Democracy to victory. His bold liberalisation of the economy was hailed as a model. Angolan President Joseph Edwardo Dos Santos's pro-Soviet stance saw him being locked in a decade-long civil war against a US-sponsored rebel force in Jonas Savimbi's Union for the Total Liberation of Angola.

Each of the changes was hailed by the US administration and aid was channelled to them, making it impossible for a country in trouble to resist. Simply put, the United States made it difficult for countries to make independent choices while lightening the burden for those that submitted to a course that served American interests.

Democratisation, as propagated by the United States, was an illusion. It was used only as a tool to remove strong leaders who stood opposed to her policies, while dictatorship was welcome as long it served her interests. Governments were compelled to privatise key and strategic infrastructure, which only big capital-rich companies from the West could take advantage of.

As Angola's Dos Santos changed his pro-Soviet stance and opened his country's oil industry to the United States, the rebel movement was dumped with the establishment of diplomatic relations in 1993,[15] and to date Dos Santos is the longest serving national leader in southern Africa, having led his country since 1979. On the other hand, Zimbabwe's Robert Mugabe has moved from darling to villain throughout his leadership, depending on the choices he made. As a darling from 1980 to 1993, he had set the standards for Mandela and others by his policy of reconciliation with whites at independence in 1980. But from that point on, he was a villain, perceived to be pursuing a one-party state as he redistributed land to the black majority. Emerging younger leaders like Fredrick Chiluba of Zambia, Joachim Chissano of Mozambique, and Morgan Tsvangirai of Zimbabwe became the darlings of the West because of what it stood to gain.

To illustrate that this was a well-planned strategy, President George H. W. Bush, in an evidently public security gaffe, revealed a secret to journalists in 1992–the year he lost an election. Bush, who was at the time referred to as a "foreign policy" president in reference to his poor economic performance and preoccupation with foreign affairs, had just returned from the Middle East, only to be met by a hostile press. He was asked why he was busy globe-trotting while his country's economy was on fire. In a frantic effort to defend his tattered record, he angrily reacted by stating that he had done much for his country. When the media did not accept that response and pressed him harder, out came the secret: he boldly proclaimed that he had liberated Eastern Europe and Africa, and that his people must now go and conquer those markets. I saw this interview live on CNN and could not believe what I heard. For the first time, my eyes were opened.

Although I could not find the transcript of Bush's exact quote, the following references in other speeches corroborate this strategy:

---

15 *Wikipedia*, "Angola-United States Relations," accessed May 2012, http://en.wikipedia.org/wiki/Angola%E2%80%93United_States_relations.

Now, make no mistake about it, now we must stay involved overseas to lead in economic restructuring for free and fair trade, open markets all over the world.[16]

As these four have told you, our economic growth depends on free markets, and our trade agreements have got to open up these markets.[17]

Also, consider Bush's remarks to the American Farm Bureau Federation in Kansas City, Missouri:

Open markets are the key to our economic future, both for American agriculture and business. That fight is going to take time, and lots of people will want immediate results. This new world of opportunity isn't going to happen overnight. But I can tell you this: Empty-headed rhetoric won't get us there. Hard work, savvy, experienced negotiation, and confidence in ourselves will get us there, proud and strong. We won the cold war, and we will win the competitive wars. We will do it on the merits, and we're going to do it the American way, through grit, through determination, and through quality.

My trip to Asia was an important and successful step toward building that new world, not with just Japan but with the whole world. We reached dozens of new agreements on market openings, from computers to paper to glass to automotive products. In Japan alone our negotiators reached 49 standard agreements in nonautomotive industries and hammered out marketing opening

16 George Bush, "Public Papers, 1992 January," *George Bush Presidential Library and Museum*, 13 January 1992, accessed July 2012, http://bushlibrary.tamu.edu/research/public_papers.php?id=3838&year=1992&month=01.

17 George Bush, "Public Papers, March 1991," *George Bush Presidential Library and Museum*, March 1991, accessed July 2012, http://bushlibrary.tamu.edu/research/public_papers.php?id=2762&year=1991&month=3.

agreements in a variety of industrial sectors. And that was just a start.[18]

And next week I'll travel to Asia to fight for open markets and more opportunities for American workers because exports abroad mean more jobs right here at home. Let there be no mistake, my number-one priority is jobs and economic growth. And I'm confident that we will succeed.[19]

Bush's statements shaped my understanding of global market politics. It is this understanding that enabled me to successfully predict the current recession in April 2000, about ten years before it commenced. After the United States successfully pushed through ESAP policies, the conquest of our markets began. The results of this blatant US strategy and the effects of markets on economic growth are only too apparent in the instant global shift in economic fortunes that took place soon thereafter.

While trade liberalisation shut down our industries amid cheers by ignorant nationals, at exactly the same time US economic fortunes shifted from recurrent recessions to the biggest and longest economic boom, which put the United States on top of the world. No single phenomenon could explain this diametrical shift in fortunes other than the fact that trade liberalisation had given new markets to the West.

Larry Diamond alluded to that in December 2008, when he wrote:

> Finally, an explosion of freedom in the early '90s liberated Eastern Europe and spread democracy from Moscow to Pretoria. Old assumptions–that democracy required Western values, high levels of education and a large middle class–crumbled. Half of sub-Saharan Africa's 48 states became democracies, and of the world's poorest countries, about two in every five are democracies

---

18   George Bush, "Public Papers, 1992 January," *George Bush Presidential Library and Museum*, January 1992, accessed July 2012, http://bushlibrary.tamu.edu/research/public_papers.php?id=3838&year=1992&month=01.

19   George Bush, "Public Papers, 1991," *George Bush Presidential Library and Museum*, 1991, accessed July 2012, http://bushlibrary.tamu.edu/research/public_papers.php?id=3789&year=1991&month=all.

today. This great shift coincided with an unprecedented moment of U.S. military, economic and cultural dominance.[20]

Coincidence or deliberate strategy? It is this "coincidence" and "unprecedented economic dominance" that needs to be understood. In my view, rather than a coincidence–as was the public view–this was a deliberate strategic initiative promulgated by the Bush administration. Why is democracy a vital US national interest that the administration has to enforce with military power? "Vital" implies that its absence is life threatening to the United States. For anything to be of national interest in the United States, it has to be underpinned by layers of academic and strategic understanding.

Zimbabwe has not fully understood that ESAP was a strategic mistake that benefited its economic adversaries at the expense of its own industries. This lack of understanding perpetuates the notion that our country's problems are due only to our politics and sanctions. This distracts her from the real issues. But, more importantly, the "educated citizens" have still not understood the self-interested economic premise behind US support for democracy and liberal political forces.

While the players are still alive, we must address the question, "Who led the charge into ESAP?" Certainly, it was not the politicians but the private sector itself. During the debates on ESAP, I attended a private-sector luncheon hosted for Professor Jeffrey D. Sachs, director of the Earth Institute at Columbia University, in Harare's Sheraton Hotel. Sachs was touring several African countries, admonishing them to adopt ESAP or suffer dire economic consequences.[21]

History will record that, on this fateful day, only one man stood up and openly opposed ESAP. It was Professor Yash Tandon,[22] who exploded in anger and made an embarrassing scene at the luncheon, as

---

20 Larry Diamond, "How to Save Democracy," *Newsweek*, 2008, accessed July 2012, http://www.newsweek.com/2008/12/30/how-to-save-democracy.html.

21 Earth Institute, "Articles," *Earth Institute Columbia University*, accessed August 2012, http://www.earth.columbia.edu/articles/view/1770.

22 Professor Yash Tandon, a Ugandan citizen, worked for Southern African Political and Economic Series (SAPES) Trust and as director of the South Centre Secretariat in Geneva, an intergovernmental policy think tank for developing countries.

he fumed, shouted, and heckled Sachs, accusing him of misleading our people. At that embarrassing moment, during which Sachs was visibly shaken and shocked to deadly silence, one Colonel David Chiweza was very embarrassed to find himself the only person in the audience applauding Tandon's remarks.

Yash Tandon was one of few voices whose thoughts resonated with me. We became friends from that day on, and this relationship did much to encourage the development of my economic thesis. As an observer, I note that time has vindicated this man and others, along with President Mugabe, who was reported to be reluctant to adopt ESAP to the point of being isolated.

The private sector led the charge, but after having cajoled political leadership to adopt ESAP, it was quick to dump that same leadership when it started failing. Corruption and economic mismanagement were suddenly given pre-eminence, as though they had assumed new proportions. The growing disquiet in the nation became fertile ground for the emergence of a new political force. Since then, the private sector has not prospered in real terms, as it was suddenly at the centre of a political turmoil it had created and fermented through its strategic errors. Will the private sector take stock and admit its own failures, or will it continue to pass blame? Only time will tell.

I trust you will agree with me that it was the opening of markets in Eastern Europe and Africa that translated into an economic boom for the United States. The evidence is there. They exported and we imported. We ran a massive trade deficit, and they ran surpluses. We closed our companies while they opened theirs. We lost our jobs while they created new ones at home. We got our political leadership condemned while Bill Clinton enjoyed a glorious reputation. We messed up our politics. They mended theirs.

It is necessary to restate the obvious: markets are the key determinant of company growth and, consequently, national economic growth. In the words of Michael E. Porter, "It is firms not nations that compete in international markets."[23] Our companies failed, and as a result, Zimbabwe failed too. But it is our country's political and private-sector

---

23   Michael E. Porter, *The Competitive Advantage of Nations* (New York: The Free Press, 1990).

leadership that collectively failed to foresee the challenges of ESAP and to defend national interests when they still had the chance.

Another invaluable lesson is that strategy is superior to macro- and microeconomic management. America did not address her problems through fiscal and monetary policies, which our economists seem to dwell on. It was strategy that delivered for the United States. It is also strategy that will deliver for Zimbabwe. In the decades that have passed, successive ministers of finance have come out with elaborate fiscal and monetary policy statements, but they all failed to change the situation.

To be successful, fiscal and monetary policies need to rest on a good strategy. Yet the lack of harmony between strategy and economic policy measures has been quite glaring. While the ESAP strategy clearly failed and has been denounced, Zimbabwe remains stuck in it. The basic principles of ESAP remain entrenched in our economic management long after we have, in theory, officially abandoned the programme. As long as markets remain liberalised to the detriment of local companies, as long as it is wrong for governments to protect their companies, and as long as government interference is loathed, we are still under the rule of ESAP. Our government has failed to correct the huge trade deficit because it remains wed to trade liberalisation ideology. It believes that companies, as if by a magic wand, will suddenly export more. To the contrary, magic is not the answer, as the US government has shown. Through aggressive, strategic, and calculated decisions, it forced open new markets in which to sell its products.

CHAPTER 6

China's Emergence as a New Global Economic Power

WE CAN NOW RELATE the principle of substitution that played out at the regional level in the 1990s to the current US-Europe and Asian situation. No country can get global economics right without getting the microeconomics right. It is small victories by companies that aggregate into national competitiveness. Therefore, as leadership neglects corporate competitiveness, it also inflicts injury upon itself. In the decade 2000–2010, the decisive nature of markets played out on a global scale. This period was marked by China's emergence as the most competitive manufacturer in the world. After dumping protectionist policies, China redirected trade traffic back to the United States, using the same "free-market bridge."

China's huge trade surplus is producing negative effects similar to those experienced in Zimbabwe. The United States, misguided by her consumerism and free-markets dogma, closed expensive producing factories at home. She assumed that her economy could still grow by producing cheaply in China and selling back home. Instead, she transferred jobs and technology to China at alarming rates. Although debate and warnings of the consequences of outsourcing production to cheaper countries started in the '80s, successive US administrations seemed powerless to reverse the trend. With the boom of the '90s reaping profits, the subject was taken out of the national agenda. However, with the return of the recession, this debate is gathering momentum again. At USD14 trillion, the United States has become the world's largest debtor nation.

Meanwhile, China's unstoppable production machine reversed the competitive dominance the United States enjoyed during the 1992–2000 era. Feeling the pressure, US companies began to sell off to emerging Chinese corporations. For example, the renowned personal computer manufacturing company, IBM, threw in the towel and sold to China's Lenovo. This is the period during which free trade began to bite the United States back. In turn, the United States is now crying foul–not because there is anything wrong with what China is doing, but because its free-market rhetoric is biting back.

I use the expression "free-market rhetoric" because it has never had a universal application. It has always been the choice expression of the superior economy. It is akin to Manny Pacquiao, the world boxing champion, challenging a novice like me to fight; I surely cannot win, but I still must fight. If the free-markets doctrine is not unfair, why do we have weight categories in boxing? Have we not been enraged when a fat predator feeds on hapless nestlings? In the post-US dominance, it is China that has taken on the mantle of predator. Before, that title belonged to the United States.

Now that the United States is competitively the weaker opponent, can she suddenly make a public foreign policy U-turn in order to protect herself? Indications are that she is slowly moving towards a new policy of cooperative trade. Unlike the powerless nation of Zimbabwe, the United States is now seeking advantages through negotiation. The call for the devaluation of the Chinese currency, and complaints about trade imbalances, dumping, and other human rights issues, are aimed at regaining its former economic advantage and extracting favourable economic concessions.

While it is clear that China has taken markets from the West, this fact is concealed from the general public because it exposes Western weaknesses. Instead, industrial decline in the West is masked in generic terminology such as global recession or financial crisis. If this were a global recession, why are the BRICS countries' economies growing? Real economic growth happens at the corporate level, and no political or foreign policy façade will erode that position. The West is in economic decline. The playing field has been altered, and the West no longer has markets for its expensive goods.

The lesson we draw from all this is this: he who has the markets is king. If a nation cannot secure markets abroad, it must, of necessity, secure them at home. The United States can still be a happy and peaceful nation as a closed economic system. However, if opening up an economic system destabilises the internal environment, then it defeats the purpose of economics, which is to create an environment or eco-system that promotes good life for its people. Take the example of the historic battles for pastures. Why give your pastures away freely, leaving your own cattle without grass to feed on, as if the victors will give back some of their cattle for free? Instead, the victims are condemned and ridiculed as incompetent. Companies, like cattle, feed on markets. The conclusion is thus: "You must keep your pastures in order to keep your cattle alive."

The debate on markets poses questions about the rights of nations to shape their destinies. The threat to this right is that some bilateral and multilateral agreements bind member states, regardless of the deleterious effects on their economic systems. Weaker nations have not been able to negotiate positions that suit their strategic objectives. Instead, economic agreements are structured to benefit the stronger nations. Unlike weaker nations, strong nations like the United States have been able to stand up and refuse to sign treaties that disadvantage them.

Even with such open free-trade agreements, covert trade battles are being fought under the pretext of retaliation for the misconduct of other nations. For example, the US-China currency dispute has led to mutual anti-dumping duties levied against products produced in both countries. Smaller nations, on the contrary, watch and do nothing while their markets are decimated. It is necessary to restore national rights so all countries can choose what their citizens may import.

What could a small nation like Zimbabwe lose if it refused to allow imports? The growing pressure to industrialise and give people a better standard of living will force small nations to disconnect their

economic systems from the world. When that happens, it will hurt all nations that depend on global markets for growth. It becomes necessary, therefore, that each nation be mindful of the impact of its policies on the prosperity of other nations.

CHAPTER 7

The Role of Markets in Industrial Growth

Let us examine Zimbabwe's own economic history and see the correlation between markets and the growth of industry. In the period 1965–1979, Rhodesia, which was then under British-imposed sanctions, was virtually a captive market for domestic companies. Feeding her companies on this small market, she was able to grow a sophisticated manufacturing industry that produced thousands of different kinds of products, with almost all of her companies being founded in this era.

Although these market conditions were imposed through British-led international sanctions after Rhodesia broke away from the United Kingdom in 1965, the resultant captive market became the foundation of her industry. The availability of this domestic market mitigated all other economic negatives, such as financial and trade embargoes and raging guerrilla warfare. In fact, the conditions, albeit imposed externally, became an economic opportunity that enabled higher levels of domestic investment than at any time in the country's development history.

Contrast this with Zimbabwe's post-independence performance during the years 1980–1989, during which the country went through years of economic stagnation. The new government inherited the

Rhodesia-era economic regulation policies. It achieved phenomenal growth in social services, such as education and health. Up to this point, the government had done reasonably well. *The Economist's*[24] 1990 anniversary cover story summed it all up with this headline: "Zimbabwe 10 Years Later, There Were More Ups Than Downs."

However, the overall productivity of the economy failed to grow. Logic entails that the economy should have continued on the same growth path, but as history records, it stagnated for a decade, neither declining nor growing. You may wonder why this stagnation occurred, when the pre-independence captive market conditions had not changed after Rhodesia became Zimbabwe on 18 April 1980.

During the 1980s, the country lagged behind in technology and consumer trends. For example, there were only a limited number of car models that could be imported, mostly French and Japanese. While the colour television was already on foreign markets, they were rarely found in the country. Only immigrants and people being sent one from friends from abroad had access to them. The country itself had stopped being creative enough to give citizens acceptable choices. The challenges of a regulated economy began to show.

Productivity was declining despite the market being so good that you could cut a stick from a tree and sell it. Diplomats who returned from abroad with a Mercedes-Benz could resell it for a fortune. Foreign products fetched as much as two or three times their original price on the local market. Entrepreneurship in Zimbabwe had died.

Entrepreneurship is one of the critical factors of production. Yes, there can be abundant markets, but without entrepreneurship those markets cannot be serviced. To fully understand the death of the country's entrepreneurship, let us analyse the demographic migration that took place with the advent of Zimbabwean independence in 1980.

Firstly, black majority rule, coming on the back of a bitter war, scared the mainly white entrepreneurs out of the country. Many white entrepreneurs, fearing a black government or simply being intolerant of black leadership, quickly migrated to other countries, with South Africa and Australia being the major destinations. Among the black

---

24 "Zimbabwe 10 Years Later: There Were More Ups Than Downs," *The Economist*, 14 April 1990.

population, there were no known entrepreneurs who owned and managed manufacturing companies. Through the 1934 Industrial Conciliation Act,[25] the Rhodesian government had passed laws that restricted black advancement. Consequently, at independence, blacks had risen only to clerical and supervisory jobs in both the private and public sectors of the country. Therefore, the only experienced entrepreneurs and managers were whites, and they emigrated in droves, leaving the inexperienced, untrained, and largely uneducated blacks to take over.

Figure 2: Zimbabwe's Migration Pattern[26]

Year	Immigrants	Emigrants	Net Migration
1972	13,966	5,150	+ 8,816
1973	9,433	7,750	+ 1,683
1974	9,649	9,050	+ 599
1975	12,425	10,500	+ 1,925
1976	7,782	14,854	- 7,072
1977	5,730	16,638	- 10,908
1978	4,360	18,069	- 13,709
1979	3,416	12,973	- 9,557

Source: Monthly Migration and Tourist Statistics (Salisbury: Central Statistical Office, 1972–1979); Annual Reports of the Commissioner of the British South African Police, 1972–1979.

Figure 2 above shows the war time migration pattern up to independence in 1980. Worthy of note is that the authors went on to comment, "High levels of white emigration continued into the independence period. An estimated 20,534 people, mostly whites, left the country in 1981, fleeing the incoming black government. Between 1980 and 1984, net migration losses exceeded 10,000 annually despite the fact that there were many black Zimbabweans returning from exile.

---

25 New African, "Why Mugabe Is Right: These Are the Facts," June 2000, accessed August 2011, http://www.raceandhistory.com/historicalviews/2000/june.html.

26 Jonathan Crush and Daniel Tevera, eds., *Zimbabwe's Exodus, Crisis, Migration, Survival* (International Development Centre, 2010).

By 1987, there were only 110,000 whites left, approximately half of the white population in 1980." Figure 3 shows that the white population declined as the war raged from 1976 to 1979, reversing the previous annual increases. The trend continued up to the introduction of ESAP in 1993.

On the other hand, the burgeoning civil service lured the few educated novices to newly created positions, leaving the private sector virtually devoid of entrepreneurship potential. The scale of job migration is further illustrated by the growth of the civil service, which saw the army increase from 10,800[27] men to 80,000 men at its peak; teachers increased from 20,000 to over 100,000 at a time when the education system was producing far fewer graduates than were needed in the economy. This expansion was similar in the health sector, where the nursing profession more than quadrupled.

These were the times when anyone with an Ordinary Level Certificate of Education (eleventh grade) could land a management job: a higher position than they ever imagined. For example, I became a battalion commander in January 1981, being called to lead more than a thousand men and equipment, well before my twenty-first birthday. Almost all the commanders up to army level were in their early twenties. In a country with an obvious educational bottleneck, the few educated were either absorbed by the civil service or quickly filled vacant private-sector jobs.

Many received accelerated promotion from supervisory management into management positions left vacant by whites. Then suddenly these novices were earning incomes and enjoying benefits that made them feel that they had arrived. This was that era of tasting executive powers, cars, moving into amazing white suburbs, fun, and satisfaction. It is no wonder that, in this euphoria, there was an entrepreneurship vacuum that could not be filled. As the saying goes, a satisfied need ceases to motivate, and true to the form, the result was lack of creativity by the nation's critical and productive age group, leading to economic stagnation.

However, this human migration was not the only cause of economic stagnation. Apart from the historical handicap in the black population,

---

27 *Wikipedia*, "Rhodesian Security Forces," accessed 15 August 2011, http://en.wikipedia.org/wiki/Rhodesian_Security_Forces.

the new and enlarged civil service demanded greater financial support and drained investment funds from the private sector. More importantly, the government put a priority on public-sector investment in social services, which marked arguably the greatest success story in Zimbabwe's social development, with new hospitals, schools, housing, and infrastructure built to improve the social status of the black people. By 1990, Zimbabwe had earned world acclaim in education and health; the country had the highest literacy rates in Africa. This of course had come at the expense, in part, of private-sector growth.

Except for the country's leadership, the majority did not see it that way. All they wanted were luxury goods, which were missing on the market. The answer to that problem did not present an opportunity to local entrepreneurs. Rather, they demanded the liberalisation that would provide the imported goods they wanted.

However, at the leadership level there was some clarity. In 1990, Vice President Joshua Nkomo was challenging me and others to quit diplomatic service and return home to do business, arguing, "You are letting the white boys do whatever they want with your country." When I made the excuse that I was only a civil servant, he told us that we were the ones that had the exposure the country needed to progress. Of course, had we all agreed on the need for entrepreneurship, and had the country agreed, the strategy would have been different. Instead, the majority fell for the liberalisation of markets in order to access trendy goods that the country's native industry had failed to provide, leading to the ESAP.

2000-2009:
The Era of Political Turmoil and Smart Sanctions

The decline of Zimbabwe's manufacturing industry left millions of people unemployed and virtually living on the streets. The government's massive investment in education did not help either, as hundreds of thousands of graduates were being churned into the job market annually, with few positions available. With no jobs, politicians came under the spotlight.

The political landscape took a new twist. Many who had recently left universities were rightfully asking, "With no jobs in the city and no land for subsistence farming, how do you want me to earn a living? Am I a bird that I should live in a tree?" The ground was fertile for land reform, and it was the people who started the land invasions, while the government, which had largely followed the policy of a negotiated land resettlement programme, was left with no choice but to stand with the people. A political turmoil ensued, leading to the imposition of smart sanctions.

You may then say, "Your theory of captive markets worked for Rhodesia under sanctions, and you have explained why it didn't work from 1980 to 1992. Why, then, did it fail when smart sanctions were imposed?"

In theory, sanctions create an ecosystem that has conditions for growth similar to those in Rhodesia during the years 1965–1980. However, smart sanctions and Rhodesian-era sanctions are completely different. Smart sanctions are an attack on the factors of production and are more deadly when compared to traditional sanctions. Rhodesian sanctions were like a blockade that prevented exports and imports. The country, consequently, had to develop and rely on an internal economic system. That system allowed Rhodesia to make choices about what she could import through its dependence on apartheid South Africa for sanctions busting. Hence, she could be selective in what to import instead of having a liberal environment that allowed consumers to make choices.

This condition became critical and necessary for managing scarce resources and maintaining a healthy balance of trade that helped stabilise the country's currency. The principle is simple: when resources are scarce, centralise management; when they are plenty, decentralise. In Rhodesia, scarce financial resources were centralised and prioritised for investment into import substitution. This position mitigated the capital and market challenges of the Rhodesian economy. In practice, the policy favoured domestic industries in accessing domestic markets. Shortfalls in the market were met through import licenses, while surpluses were exported. The licenses were used to control the quantum of imports in order to avoid crowding out local companies' markets. Self-reliance was so important that consumers were compelled to settle for homemade black-and-white televisions while, next door, South Africa was awash with luxurious colour televisions.

In 2001, the United States imposed smart sanctions on Zimbabwe following the controversial compulsory land redistribution programme. The United States and the EU opposed the fast track land reform programme as being an authoritarian attempt to roll back the advance of democracy in the country. In order to put pressure on the Zimbabwe government and help advance opposition interests, the United States passed the Zimbabwe Democracy and Economic Recovery Act (S. 494).[28] Under the bill, the United States would vote against any advance of financial assistance and credit lines to Zimbabwe from the IMF, World Bank, and other institutions. In addition, the United States imposed sanctions on key institutions and individuals that were seen to be working with and assisting the government of Zimbabwe. The US financial system was generally prevented from advancing loans to Zimbabwean companies. There was a list of strategic government and private-sector individuals who were barred from travelling. These measures, which were dubbed "Smart Sanctions," were also adopted by the EU. However, like deadly smart bombs, the nickname was fatally deceptive.

In the public's view, they looked like they were more humane and less harmful than full sanctions. They were apparently only targeted at the discredited government, its leadership, and collaborators while the citizens seemed to be spared, because they were still free to travel and import whatever they wanted. What was hidden from the public was that, from a systems theory point of view, the sanctions dismembered the economic system by attacking capital, markets, and leadership subsystems. Indeed, like smart bombs, they do not look "ugly," yet they are the deadliest sanctions the regime ever conceived. More importantly, they attack markets and, by their design, exacerbate the flight of capital, thereby drying up critical capital markets; hence the misnomer "smart."

Unlike economic blockades and trade embargoes that isolate an entire economic system, they attack the critical success factors of an economic system, rendering it incapable of functioning. They are surgical and yet crippling. By isolating leadership, you decapitate and paralyse the nerve centre; by preventing the flow of capital, you stop all

---

28 *Wikipedia*, "Zimbabwe Democracy and Economic Recovery Act of 2001," accessed February 2012, http://en.wikipedia.org/wiki/Zimbabwe_Democracy_and_Economic_Recovery_Act_of_2001.

investment and productive activity; by encouraging citizens to continue to import freely, you not only encourage them to waste scarce foreign currency on nonproductive consumption, but you also accelerate the flight of capital. In other words, if you simultaneously cut off financial inflows into a country while allowing citizens to export the little currency available through uncontrolled trade, you financially haemorrhage the economy to the point of mimicking death by asphyxia.

This is a deadly assault on the economic system that results in sanctions hurting not only the politicians but also the people themselves. They are truly smart—not as in clean but as in clever, neat, and efficient, because they are able to do the damage while hiding the weapon. Smart sanctions are a public-relations coup because the victims cannot see the weapon and cannot react appropriately.

To illustrate my point, old-fashioned bombs attracted public outcry against the civility of the bombers. The outrage looked something as horrific as the 9/11 bombing, and yet the smart bombs look as innocent as the post-9/11 cumulative costs in lives and resources when fighting the war. In summary, smart sanctions are blocking capital inflows while ensuring that the little that trickles in is wasted through consumerism. Imports continue to sap the markets for local industry, while industry is starved of capital to retool and compete effectively. The result is the opposite of what traditional sanctions produce, because they isolate the entire self-existing economic system.

To summarise this chapter, let us understand that markets consistently determined the economic fortunes of Zimbabwe. A lack of entrepreneurship influenced the economic stagnation of the decade 1980–1990, while ESAP policies wiped out markets for domestic industry from 1992 to date. Smart sanctions have added another dimension, in the flight of capital from the economy in addition to market challenges.

In 1981, before my twenty-first birthday, I was promoted to a high managerial position (like many Zimbabweans). Here I am seen with my officers at the 35 Infantry Battalion Field Firing Range in Chipinge.

Professor Yash Tandon sharply disagreed with Professor Geoffrey Sachs on Economic Structural Adjustment Programmes.

Here I am toasting with Chinese Minister of Defence General Qin Jiwei at a function.

Zimbabwe's Vice President Joshua Nkomo challenged enlightened citizens to return home and be engaged in private-sector business. Here I am on his far right during talks with Chinese leaders. On his near right is Ambassador Boniface Chidyausiku and Air Marshal Perence Shiri.

We enjoyed excellent working relations with all countries. Here I am relaxing with Brazilian, Japanese, and American attachés after a morning game of tennis.

CHAPTER 8

The Foundations of the Chinese Economic Miracle: A Personal Experience

To demonstrate the correlation between economic success and climatic conditions caused by the factors of production, let us examine how China rapidly industrialised under economic conditions that resembled the Rhodesian-era sanctions. In 1979, China announced that she was liberalising her economy by opening it to the outside world, reversing the policies of the Cultural Revolution, a thirty-year period during which she isolated herself from the outside world. During that period, China was a self-existing economic system, where all five factors of production were available.

After China became Communist in 1949, it enacted a land reform law. The 1950 law banned ownership of land by landlords and transferred small pieces of land to the peasant population. Land was seized and redistributed to all the people en masse, where nearly 310 million people were involved in carrying out land reform and around 300 million peasants were assigned 47 million hectares of land, together with farm implements, livestock, and buildings.[29] This redistribution exercise increased production and is believed to have laid the foundation for China's economic development. The most important contribution was freeing people from being slaves and abolishing the landlord system. Families were given pieces of land (some as small as 1.3 acres). This availability and access were key factors in allowing as many people as possible to participate in economic development, as masters and not as slaves.

China's self-reliance, production, and consumption enabled her to develop technology in all aspects of life. This became an advantage for her, as she is competent in a multitude of technology areas. The domestic environment provided unchallenged market opportunities for her industries. Unlike Rhodesia's situation, China had excommunicated herself from the outside world. One result of a closed economic system was the existence of rudimentary and outdated technology.

Just one example. When I arrived in China in 1988, I was shocked to see matchboxes and match sticks that were different from those in Africa. The makers simply went into the bush, cut some twigs to size, and dipped their heads in some incendiary substance, and there you are, you had a functioning match. And the box was made of raw, unprocessed wood, with the strike patch pasted on the side. This was a nuclear power that was not even processing its matches! The difference with Africa was that match making was a mystery, since they were made in the factory. Ordinarily people would not have a clue as to how to make a basic one, even with sticks. That means that unlike Zimbabweans, Chinese technology, however crude, was now in the loins of the people and just waiting for machines to be perfected. The sheer simplicity of Chinese matches was enlightening; I had an "aha" experience. Was making matches that simple? They even suggested I could do it at home.

The process of getting technology into the hands of the people is important. The Chinese were committed to producing everything for themselves as a first step. They produced poor-quality goods that became the sacrifices and the social cost of inculcating technology into people. The fruit of that approach is the miracle economy she enjoys

---

29   History Learning Site, *China 1949 to 1953*, accessed 11 October 2011, http://www.historylearningsite.co.uk/china_1949_to_1953.htm.

today. With basic technology in her people, economic reforms were not a matter of opening borders to a flood of Western goods. Rather, China focused on re-establishing cultural and technological exchanges with the outside world, while keeping her markets to herself. In short, China adopted a phased approach, which protected, rather than destroyed, her economic system. Quite the opposite of what happened in Zimbabwe.

I arrived in China nine years after her open-door policy began, but I found her economic system remained very much closed. The conditions I experienced point to the value of having all five factors of production present.

First, China was using two currencies. All Chinese citizens used the People's (Renmimbi) Yuan as the currency. The Foreign Exchange Certificate (FEC) Yuan was the currency used by foreigners. When tourists, expatriates, diplomats, and official visitors came into the country, they would take their currency into the bank and exchange it for FEC, which was the only currency they were supposed to use while in China.

The object of this policy was capital accumulation. It was not easily available, and the Chinese demonstrated a disciplined commitment to mobilising, safeguarding, and deploying it efficiently. The Chinese used this policy as a mousetrap to capture foreign currency that foreigners brought in the country. These inflows, together with export revenue, were leveraged as domestic investment capital long before foreign investment started to play a bigger role in the country.

In contrast with Chinese policy, Zimbabwe is trading on the domestic market in foreign currency. This is tying down capital that could be deployed into productivity. Zimbabwe, with her perennial trade deficits, is a net exporter of foreign currency. Since she is unable to print her own currency, this means there is no currency for domestic trade.

Unlike Zimbabwe, China's domestic market was monopolised by domestic companies. To illustrate this, there were no foreign products in the mainstream economy. The trickle of foreign products found in the economy were provided exclusively for foreigners and were sold in "friendship" stores, one per city, located in each of the major cities, such as Beijing and Shanghai (cities with at least ten million people).

As the name implies, these stores were a means of keeping China "friendly" to foreigners, who were used to trendy goods and groceries. These shops, the size of an average Zimbabwean supermarket, served the diplomatic and expatriate community with international groceries. Armed police guarded the entrance to a friendship store, and only foreigners and overseas Chinese (the equivalent of a returning Diaspora) were admitted by way of passports or diplomatic cards. Everywhere else, there were no foreign products, not even a Coke or a foreign beer.

In addition to friendship stores, there was a diplomatic shop in Beijing that sold international brands of home appliances to the foreign community and overseas Chinese living in China. With this policy, China deliberately promoted domestic markets to her companies. The quality or cost of the local goods did not matter. "Made in China" was the only qualification.

Foreign products were introduced into special economic zones that China used as pilot projects to experiment on trade liberalisation policies before they were extended to the rest of the country. In special economic zones, such as Shenzhen, foreigners were allowed to invest and sell only within the economic zone, or else they had to export the products. It is in those economic zones that foreign companies like McDonald's and Kentucky Fried Chicken first set foot. Local Chinese needed permits to travel to special economic zones, as these were virtual foreign territories carved out within their country. This way the Chinese experimented with economic liberalisation while keeping their domestic markets intact.

China was interested in the accumulation of knowledge. Quality and price considerations were secondary. To think that China's domestic radio industry in 1988 was far behind Zimbabwe's is unimaginable. Zimbabwe's World Radio Systems and ZECO produced far more durable radios with better sound quality than Chinese radios. The only Chinese radio I bought at that time lasted a month. Outwardly it looked flashy, with a lot of colour and lights.

While locally manufactured goods were plentiful, the Chinese government admitted there was a problem with quality; in a famous quality campaign, it dumped what it called "shoddy goods" into the sea. Simply put, the Chinese government had been deliberately patient and tolerant of poor quality since opening to the outside world. She was signalling that experimentation was up, and it was time to catch up with the rest of the world.

One could clearly see that the Chinese had the basic skills and knowledge needed to make anything. What they needed to improve was their quality. This is where they got it right. They were always quick to spot centres of excellence and use them as best practice and benchmarks for improvement. If some person or institution did well, they would be publicly cited as a national "model." That meant they set the standard for the nation to imitate.

On the international scene, "American Standard" was the benchmark, not Japanese. America (called "Mei Guo" in Chinese, meaning "Beautiful Country") was a dream of every Chinese person on the street. If they wanted to convince you to purchase something, they would say, "This is American Standard!" The ordinary Chinese mind had its sights set on America. The leadership had long transformed its vision into the national slogan, "To surpass Britain and catch up with America by year 2025."[30] This goal could be felt through the ordinary Chinese's zeal and admiration for anything American.

In the next few years, controlled imports of foreign products began to flow in. I think this was particularly good for China because it had the effect of accelerating learning and sharpening, rather than displacing, domestic capability. She took that as an opportunity to benchmark her technology. This showed that when people have the capability to replicate new technology, they take competition as an opportunity for advancement. The imports were introduced in small doses, much like a vaccine and not an infection. Had imports not been controlled at the time, it might have resulted in a situation similar to Zimbabwe's, where liberalisation killed companies. Some measure of competition is healthy, but governments should not leave the survival of domestic industries to fate because the ultimate objective is not competition, but the economic well-being of the nation.

What was the wisdom of sacrificing quality? The Chinese government allowed the economy to effectively create "laboratory conditions" that allowed companies to make mistakes without being punished. People who do not experiment and make mistakes cannot gain mastery of knowledge. The absence of laboratory conditions requires a "get-it-right-the-first-time" approach, meaning weaker economies either pay

---

30   Liu Guogang, Liang Wensen, et al., *China's Economy in the Year 2000* (Beijing: Foreign Languages Press, 1990).

for the best imported technology in the world or remain second grade. Without capital, the best approach to accumulating capital is to build on the small successes you have locally. And that means being patient as companies make mistakes and learn from them.

Life principles demonstrate this growth model. A child who does not jump into the water cannot learn how to swim. In the same way, Chinese companies were willing to tolerate humble beginnings. In order to harden or acclimatise their companies to foreign competition, the Chinese introduced imports gradually. As companies looked at foreign products, they were simply asking themselves the question, "Can we replicate the technology?" If not, "Can we purchase it?"

Armed with their basic technology, they replicated any product they could see, and the result is an economic miracle. These were the conditions that existed in Zimbabwe during the period 1965–1990 when the economy grew. As a novice, even I was able to plunge in and venture into engineering with surprising success, until ESAP came along.

China also recognised the "law of process," which implies that development and growth is a process rather than an event. While Zimbabwe changed policy overnight, the Chinese did so gradually and thus responsibly, realising that there is a time to crawl, a time to walk, and a time to run on the journey to becoming a world champion.

Labour is another key factor in production that a state must nurture, develop, and keep in a state of good health. Labour encompasses the people themselves: how they are raised, protected, retained, and deployed for economic use. The Chinese adopted a deliberate plan to train, retain, and attract labour and entrepreneurial skills to support the development needs of the country. The measures adopted included restrictions on travelling abroad. Citizens did not have the right to passports. Only those travelling on official business would be issued temporary passports and would surrender them on return. Chinese diplomats were not to be accompanied by family members.

Figure 3: This 1998 Article Shows We Had Taken
a Dive before ESAP Overcame Us

Men who made a dream come true

DAVIBERT Engineering (Pvt) Ltd started as an idea that was nurtured over some years until fruition about two years ago.

Founded by retired Brigadier David Chiweza, who is the chief executive, the company was registered in 1991 but only began full operations in February 1996. It was formed in response to challenges from the country's political leadership for blacks to venture into business areas other than the traditional retail and transport sectors.

Brig Chiweza's interest in an engineering business had long been a dream as he had not studied engineering. He viewed the field as offering the kind of challenges he needed.

It was therefore no surprise that when a friend, then an engineer and lecturer at the University of Zimbabwe, offered to assist he took up the project.

Despite people saying that the company would soon collapse due to the harsh economic conditions created by the introduction of the Economic Structural Adjustment Programme which saw the closure of many large and small engineering companies, Davibert Engineering took root and is now up and running.

It owes its success to the perseverance, dedication and a great deal of flexibility of its management and staff. In the two years of operation the company has been able to come up with nine different types of products and has thrice changed its operational focus, giving rise to three production cells specialising in metal fabrication, machining and tube and wire products.

The general engineering side continues to offer contract engineering services to local industry, meeting both fabrication and machining requirements for a range of customers.

In production engineering, the focus is on tube and pipe products where metal furniture, trolleys and wire baskets are produced. The metal furniture range includes folding furniture.

Davibert Engineering successfully lodged two patents with the Patents Office and has had its trademark, SPESAPO, registered.

The company employs 15 workers, including a qualified engineer and several highly skilled artisans.

Said Brig. Chiweza: "The future can only be encouraging. Thanks to God we have loyal customers, a supportive bank and well wishers. We have come of age and taken off.

"There have been plenty of lessons and there are more with each day. Being able to transform materials

Not surprisingly, just as with Zimbabweans during their economic crisis, every Chinese national wanted to leave the country. They were curious and hungry for the good life enjoyed by those living abroad. It did not matter which country it was, they just wanted out. But no matter how educated they were, the Chinese government kept the educated and skilled people in the country, working for the salary equivalent of a menial labourer. It has been said that when US President George H. W. Bush demanded that China stop incarcerating its citizens, China's paramount leader, Deng Xiaoping, told him that his country was ready to release two hundred million Chinese nationals immediately if America needed them. According to the story, Bush declined the offer.

While keeping those inside under lock and key, the Chinese government was creating an incentive for the return of skilled and business-savvy Chinese nationals based overseas. On their return, they retained the special name and status of overseas Chinese to distinguish them from ordinary citizens. To protect them from the poor living standards in China, returning citizens enjoyed diplomatic privileges, immunity from China's "one child" policy, and release from all other restrictions. They received preferential treatment ahead of locals, a practice that anyone would condemn as inequality before the law. They received first priority in housing allocations, shopped in diplomatic and friendship stores, and retained their passports to travel freely. The government built recreational clubs where they took up exclusive membership away from the somewhat culturally incompatible locals.

At the same time, Chinese public television broadcast lessons on how to behave and treat foreigners well. Locals were so fascinated with these rare foreigners that they often surrounded them just to get a glimpse. On the other hand, the locals' spitting tradition was an eyesore that had to be eliminated, and the government did a good job of eliminating "spitting pots" from public places and persuading citizens to stop the practice.

The attraction of skilled labour and entrepreneurs did not just end with the overseas Chinese. There were parallel programmes for the education and training of local entrepreneurs. Foreign investors were made welcome through liberal immigration laws and special treatment. The import of these measures was to attract labour and entrepreneurship. These measures also served to create seed technology in the nation, just as one sows a seed variety. The Chinese viewed foreign entrepreneurs as assets and not as a nuisance. When these people set up their enterprises, they transferred knowledge to the locals, who soon imitated the technology on a wide scale. The value of these skills was demonstrated when Western and other countries competed to woo skilled workers from Hong Kong before the former British colony returned to China. Canadian and Australian governments sent scouts to assess potential immigrants who met their skill and investment criteria. Such measures, coupled with generous living conditions, can help increase investment and technology in a country.

China's industrialisation did not start with great inflows of investment capital. She had to create an economic environment that held the promise for investment returns. According to the *1990–1991 Defence and Foreign Affairs Handbook*,[31] China's annual export proceeds in 1988 were USD57.1 Bn, while imports amounted to USD52 Bn– this being the little foreign exchange earnings to support 1.1 billion people.

The difference between China and Zimbabwe is that the former maintained a healthy balance of payments position, while diligently investing all foreign exchange earnings in the productive sector. Apart from the fact that she maintained a favourable balance of trade, China deliberately leveraged her export earnings for industrial growth through the exclusive import of advanced tools, machinery, and technology.

China's major imports were grain, fertiliser, steel, coal, machinery, and industrial products, raw materials, and equipment. This trend of shrewd management of exports and imports still remains. In 2008, 88 per cent of China's import bill went to production-related products such as machinery and transport (43 per cent); textile rubber and metallurgical products (11 per cent); chemical products (11 per cent); minerals and fuel materials (11 per cent); and inedible raw materials (12 per cent), with only 12 per cent attributed to the import of non-production-related products.[32]

Simply put, China was never wasteful. She did not import all the luxury goods that Zimbabwe does, except products that support

31   Gregory Copley, *The 1990–1991 Defence and Foreign Affairs Handbook*, Reference Guide (International Media Corporation, 1989).
32   Star Mass, "China Imports and Exports", accessed 17 January 2012, http://www.starmass.com/china_review/imports_exports/china_imports_exports.htm.

tourism, which was another major foreign currency earner. China understood the importance of capital as a factor of production even before foreign capital started to flow in.

To demonstrate this commitment, in 1988, the only small cars on Chinese roads were taxis and government or corporate vehicles. All other traffic comprised utility vehicles, such as "made in China" trucks, buses, trams, bicycles, and trains. No Chinese citizen was allowed to own a private car, and no foreign vehicles were imported. It did not matter whether you were the president of an airline or some other important person; once you finished work, you left the official car and rode a bicycle.

This was a demonstration of the political will to prioritise investment ahead of consumerism. This policy saved the country billions of dollars that it could spend on essential services, created markets for domestic companies, and ensured the little foreign exchange available was applied to machinery and technology imports.

However, this huge market serviced by cheap, low-quality products became a magnet for investors. Manufacturing at these same low costs, while churning out better quality, would be especially profitable for an exporting investor. Investors are always sizing up such opportunities. If they walked into Zimbabwe and saw all the international brands imported into the country, they would conclude that there was no market, because competing with Samsung would be tough and risky.

Consequently, the easygoing environment was so attractive that investors made a beeline into China. The adverse political and human rights issues did not matter. Legend has it that, on the prompt return of foreign investors after prodemocracy forces were crushed in Tiananmen Square in June 1989, an unnamed Western reporter remarked, "The smell of money is more important than democracy and human rights."

There is no doubt that foreign capital played a big part in the latter stages of its development, as China's investment attractiveness grew. In addition to the natural investment attractions created by the opportunities inside China—including cheap labour, a big market, and a hard-working, educated, and knowledgeable workforce—China also put in place attractive investment incentives. These included tax breaks, generous remission of profits, government assistance, and special living conditions, as discussed above.

Figure 4: China Invested All Her Export Earnings in Productive Assets

China % Imports by Product in 2008

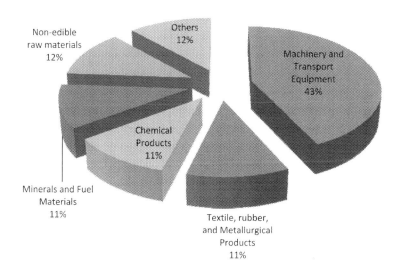

Non-edible raw materials 12%

Others 12%

Machinery and Transport Equipment 43%

Chemical Products 11%

Minerals and Fuel Materials 11%

Textile, rubber, and Metallurgical Products 11%

The Key Ingredients of the Chinese Economic Miracle

The discussion above demonstrates the discipline and commitment of the Chinese government to providing the key ingredients for an economic miracle. These ingredients are as follows:

a. Provision of the five factors of production. These factors provided the framework and climate for the key raw materials that the economy needed to function. At the same time, these ingredients had to be available and accessible to the people.

b. It was clear that China bent over backwards to attract and retain all the factors of production. In the process, she adopted policies that were quite unpalatable to the civilised world. She had a choice: to maintain the status quo or to change. She buried her head in the sand and went ahead with her policies.

c. China worked hard to attract foreign investment, but she also created the conditions that were attractive to investors. Investors want a return on their investments. As Zimbabwe seeks investment, she must think in terms of profit benefits to the investor and not just about infrastructure-related convenience.

d. China's economic model demonstrates that capital follows opportunity and exposes the myth that a country must meet all traditional political, social, and economic requirements in order to attract investment. China did not meet political and human rights standards expected of the world, and yet investors flocked there.

e. China appreciated the value of seeding technology. She welcomed skilled people and people with new technology so that her people could learn from them. Apart from attracting foreign investors who transferred technology, she also invested in technology.

f. China went through a period of broad-based production experimentation and perfecting. She understood the value of "lowering" the standard in order to allow the people to participate in mass production.

g. China took development as a process rather than an event. In contrast, Zimbabwe mistimed her policies, often treating them as events that ultimately crippled the economic system.

h. China did not invest in wasteful consumption. Even today, she continues to deploy her export earnings into productive sectors. She applied the typical "Rich Dad, Poor Dad" wisdom by Robert Kiyosaki,[33] who says liabilities are "anything that takes money out of your pocket," while assets are "properties that bring money into your pocket."

33 Robert Kiyosaki and Sharon L. Lechter, *Rich Dad Poor Dad: What the Rich Teach Their Kids about Money That the Poor and Middle Class Do Not!* (New York: Warner Books, 1997).

CHAPTER 9
The Zimbabwean Economic Context: A Contrast

Now, IN CONTRAST WITH China, we need to find out how Zimbabwe is deploying and managing the factors of production. We thus ask the question, "Is Zimbabwe really short of capital?" No. Not at all! Just by checking out the import bill, we see that it represents capital that could be leveraged for growth. At USD6.4 Bn[34] in 2011, much of that money could be substituted for investment capital and thousands of new jobs created annually. Conversely, these imports also represent market opportunities that local companies could seize.

The vehicle traffic that chokes Zimbabwe's roads is ample evidence of capital that could have been deployed into productivity to create a better tomorrow. In 2011, Zimbabwe's light vehicle imports exceeded $1 Bn. This is a large enough market to attract investment by some smaller auto companies. Mazda Zimbabwe could have grown into a dominant company ready to export cars into Africa, had that market been reserved for it. The production of a few kinds of models would

---

34 Zimbabwe Treasury, *National Budget Statement*, 2012, accessed 24 November 2012, http://www.zimtreasury.org/downloads/930.pdf.

create a supporting network of manufacturing companies and increase the amount of local materials in the cars. Unfortunately, Zimbabwe has the "luxury" of having numerous varieties of car models, crowding out the potential growth of Mazda in the country.

For a long time, the South Korean market was monopolised by its domestic auto companies, such as Hyundai and Daewoo, which provided the needed springboard for globalisation. This is the necessary strategy of getting the domestic auto company established first before it can expand globally. The idea is to create large segments of domestic markets that can be profitably serviced by a domestic company. There is no economic benefit derived from a multiplicity of car brands serving a small market, like Zimbabwe's.

The belief in the overriding precedence of consumer choice over rationality has crippled leadership and the nation at large. As I see it, leaders have largely abrogated responsibility for shaping destiny by avoiding tough decisions, fearing that such action negates democratic principles. French revolutionary Alexandre Ledru-Rollin[35] said, "There go my people. I must follow them, for I am their leader," in apparent reference to liberal leadership. Zimbabweans have been misled to believe that strong leadership is dictatorial. Leaders, fearing this tag, abrogate strategic considerations in a desperate bid to remain relevant to and popular with the people.

Limiting consumer choice contradicts today's human rights norms. It is this concept that will define the future of humankind, for this animal called human rights blocks the doorway to human freedom and life. This debate about rights has crippled many plans. Many millions have died from HIV in the name of human rights. Consumer rights obstacles stem from the failure to recognise the economy as a system. Like all systems, it must have a nerve centre, a head that makes choices in the greater interest of all the organs of the body.

In a family, there must be a "government" that decides what the family will buy. If a family is going to give the children free chequebooks to spend without control, that family will soon be broke. If, at family level, the right to spend freely is curtailed, one wonders why a state cannot make right choices for all in order to promote the commonwealth of

---

35 The Library of Congress, *Respectfully Quoted, A Dictionary of Quotations* (Barnes & Noble, 1993).

the family. We have to rethink our limiting beliefs and values. Human rights should never take precedence over scientific principles. There are many arguments, but in the final analysis, it is more righteous to make those decisions that will prevent the suffering of many for the few. The Chinese model demonstrated that resolute pursuit of the truth over human rights ultimately preserves the economic rights of many. More Chinese enjoy a higher quality of life now than they could have, had they allowed human rights obstacles to stand in the way.

Zimbabwe is also trapped in human rights obstacles, but the courage to make unpopular decisions is a necessary quality of good leadership. Truth deferred will lead to disaster, but the truth executed will always be vindicated. The paradox of wisdom and mediocrity is that wisdom, which must of necessity lead, is the domain of a few, while mediocrity, which must follow, is in the majority. Unfortunately, leaders misunderstand democracy and try to lead with majority views, which is populism. It is akin to cutting with the blunt edge of a knife. If we think democracy means the mediocrity of the majority, then how and why do Western governments lead with science, the domain of the few, and yet remain democratic? I therefore argue that in making economic decisions, comprehensive rationality should take precedence over political expedience.

Should Zimbabwe continue to decline because consumerism makes choices for the country? Should not leaders make wise choices for the people? Unless the leadership is prepared, as the Chinese were, to make wise choices for the people, the country cannot move forward. There ought to be a balance between strong and weak leadership, the extremes of which tend to become retrogressive. We can only learn this principle from the greatest democracy itself, the United States. When it comes to matters of principle, the United States has been resolute, even to the extent of spilling blood, in protecting what it calls its vital national interests. The War on Terror, whatever its outcome might be, was based on the rationale that weakness would encourage aggression, and that it was necessary to stop it even if it meant violating the lives and rights of some people. Leadership made some decisions against the popular views of the people in order to ensure that right took precedence over populism. The use of the minimum necessary force to get the job done is required of leaders. Leadership cannot be trapped in human rights if force is the answer to the problem. It is as equally wrong to use cotton in a situation that demands a hammer as it is to use a hammer to kill a fly.

Zimbabwe lacks the capital factor because she is not deploying it with wisdom. She misuses export earnings through the import of non-productive goods. While labour is plentiful, Zimbabwe has not made any visible efforts to create attractive conditions to lure skills and entrepreneurship from abroad. Instead, quite a lot of skills and entrepreneurs left the country. The white population in Zimbabwe has decreased significantly, skilled citizens who left the country remain in the world capitals, and no policy has been put in place to attract them back. Zimbabweans, used to immigrants of European descent, remain very suspicious of Asian immigrants. While there are many Asians and Chinese coming to the country, there really is no official position on what to do with immigrants and what benefits are envisioned from their arrival.

Zimbabwe has not appreciated the value that markets have for economic development. Markets remain open when its citizens are non-competitive or are incapable of accessing markets abroad. In that case, it is the foreign companies that are positioning themselves outside the borders to suck out the wealth through imports. The benefits of human development through accelerated technology transfer are not at play in the country. Unlike the Chinese, who were empowered to be economic participants, a very small per centage of the Zimbabwean population is involved in experiential industrial activities that enable learning and growth. The rest are mere spectators. For growth to begin, the people have got to start "doing."

While China demonstrated that she had an economic system, Zimbabwe's economic system is dysfunctional. It can hardly be described. An examination of its elements–land, labour, capital, entrepreneurship, and markets–reveals that not all of them serve the common goal of economic production. For example, the country's hypermarkets are parasitic in nature. Instead of serving the national system, they are serving foreign interests by preferring to consume goods produced by foreign bodies and entities. A human system would automatically reject anything that is not a part of its system. Parasites (like ticks on a dog) take from a system without contributing to the overall goals of the entire system.

Examples of such parasites are companies like Pick 'n Pay, a South

African hypermarket chain that recently set up in Zimbabwe. Nearly 95 per cent of its products are South African imports. It is a beautiful facility that easily attracts consumers. Apart from giving pleasure to consumers, it does not contribute to the economic goals of the country. Instead, it is serving the economic goals of a foreign country by distributing and promoting South African products. To correct this, it must plug into Zimbabwe's economic system by distributing on behalf of Zimbabwean companies. As mentioned earlier, Zimbabwe's commerce and trade must serve the domestic industry through distribution of local produce and management of shortfalls and surpluses through trade. This systems goal was lost, and subsystems now serve profit motives ahead of systems goals, making the entire economic system dysfunctional.

What, then, is the new dispensation? Has Zimbabwe transformed into a global system where supply and demand elements are supported and nourished by the global environment? It seems true only in ambition. Except for mineral resources, the world demands none of her manufactured products. She is not competitive enough to access world capital and markets. She is highly dependent on handouts and thus has no control of her destiny. China designed and controlled her economic system, based on domestic production and markets. China was clear about how the economy would interface with the world economy in a beneficial way. One cannot tell whether Zimbabwe's current economy is a closed system or an open system and, if open, whether it can regulate and control the bugs that come with an open environment. These are obvious systems contradictions.

As I see it, Zimbabwe needs to weld everyone together, so that leadership can drive the nation towards its destiny. A weak leadership approach, fuelled by misunderstandings of human rights and freedom, is crippling. The British thinker Edward De Borno[36] likens the lack of unity to a "shipwreck." How can a person set sail in a broken canoe without first putting the pieces together? How can one drive a stripped car? While all the car components may be present, they have to be pieced and welded together in order to steer it in a desired direction.

The unity of leadership and its people for a common purpose is what

---

36 Edward De Borno, *Lateral Thinking for Management* (New York: Harper and Row, 1970).

drives a nation forward. This remains the biggest philosophical question surrounding our notion of modern democracy. In a shipwreck situation like Zimbabwe, the system sabotages itself by keeping leadership busy trying to retrieve parts of the ship that have long set sail in different directions. No wonder that Zimbabwe is still at the same economic position as she was thirty-two years ago.

In the final analysis, economic liberalisation has strategically decapitated the economic system's head. Doctors will tell you that with any malfunction of the brain, the limbs will lose control and coordination. Military strategists will tell you that without the command and control function, the enemy is defeated. Therefore, decapitation of the command and control function of an economy is utterly destructive. It is in the nation's best interests to guard against crippling doctrines and restore the full functionality of an economic system, complete with centrally controlled subsystems.

To sum up this section, it is important to note that the life in China I described demonstrates how the Chinese government worked to provide all the five factors of production. It also demonstrates the political will of the government and a nation's willingness to make sacrifices. Lastly, it demonstrates that the Chinese government had a game plan. It was this rational plan and not populist policies that lifted China. She developed a shared economic thesis, and the stability of the Chinese government ensured that the plan would be executed. Had there been political instability, it is probable that the thesis could have been aborted midstream. While there may be elements that are unique to China, the principles that China used can be applied to any country with success. It will only depend on the national psychology.

For example, America's $14 trillion in debt can be wiped out if Americans choose to wear their own homemade shoes. They have the capacity to produce them and create employment and wealth in the process. However, they can also choose to be trapped by the belief that a made-in-China shoe is worth the pain of a recession.

In Zimbabwe, the lack of a scientifically designed economic system is evident in the lack of continuity in economic management. Because the truth cannot be amended, there should be continuity, and the nation should maintain its economic systems for decades without fundamental structural changes. Policy changes are most often a reflection of a lack of confidence in the existing economic plans. In some cases, such changes result from the lack of appreciation of the time lag between plan implementation and results. But the most disappointing aspect of it is the choice between rationality and expediency, which itself demonstrates a lack of respect for science.

In Zimbabwe, quite a number of economic choices were based on political expedience. For example, Zimbabwe has flip-flopped on its tariff policy many times, at one time increasing tariffs to protect local industry, then immediately reversing the policy at the slightest squeal of constituencies resisting the change. Since the Government of National Unity came to power in 2009, tariff policies have revolved 180 degrees. This reflects a lack of conviction in decision making. Moreover, it is a failure to understand that, once tariffs are raised, local supply response will take between twelve and twenty-four months if new plant capacity is to be installed. Unfortunately, this unpredictability makes markets unstable and creates a high risk for investors.

In order to prevent this policy flip-flop, there is need for a thesis, a constant against which change can be measured. A unit of measure is set as a constant, and everything else is measured against it. In the same way, I have coined the term "industronometer": my method of measuring the quality of an industrial climate. A proven thesis of what works for our economy is what is needed to prevent habitual changes in economic plans.

The industronometer is a tool that helps measure the correctness of an economic decision. It is based on the theory that the five factors of production–land, capital, labour, entrepreneurship, and markets–are the constants a country must have. The industronometer therefore measures the degree to which a policy or intervention increases or decreases the quality and availability of these factors. The objective is to affect them in a positive way. I proffer the view that the factors of production are vital national interests that must be defended in the best interests of the people. I briefly discuss them below:

Land

Land includes its surface as well as all the resources on or under it. Historically, land and land rights have driven nations to war. Land rights violations by other nations rob citizens, while land monopolisation by individuals and private groups has the same effect as that of an invasion. Therefore, access to land by the people is in the national interest. Land in Zimbabwe, while being state owned, must be tradable at affordable costs. While there is a ninety-nine-year lease on some of the beneficiaries of land, it is noted that some are unable to economically put it to production. There are current restrictions on selling, transferring rights, letting, subletting, or partnering others in joint ventures in resettled land. Anyone inviting partners may lose his land.

Instead, the government should encourage landowners to share land usage in creative ways. Citizens can then combine economic strengths for productive purposes in a mutually beneficial way. At present, ownership rather than production seems to be the primary concern. To prevent the emergence of new landlords and speculative land holdings, rules could be established that require land to be put to use within a specific time frame, or there will be compulsory requirements for reallocation.

Labour

Labour, in its broad national security implications, includes the health, safety, security, education, and training of our people so that they can be economically productive. Any threat to these aspects of labour will negatively affect the development of a nation. Zimbabwe's labour has the right to be employed in its own country. That means education and skills training should continue to be strengthened.

However, the most important idea from the China example is the recognition that education is not just academic. It also comes through the experiences of the people. More education takes place in the factories than in the classroom. It is therefore important to lower the technology standards so that even the novices can have a "feel of the ball." While Zimbabwe has excellent education and its people are highly literate, they have not perfected their knowledge because few ever get to practice it. There is no industry in the country, leading to millions of unemployed loitering in the streets. If markets are addressed, there will be sufficient employment opportunities that will expose people to technology and other creative ideas. Many have no idea what a factory looks like. Furthermore, our trade exhibitions attract no machinery merchants. The reality is that many entrepreneurship ideas are not invented. They are copied from others. It is said that a picture is worth a thousand words. Even the country's first billionaire, Strive Masiyiwa, did not invent the idea of a cellular network. He was an ordinary man who got the seed from a foreign country and planted it at home. Zimbabweans need exposure to technology and industry if they are to reach their fullest potential.

Capital

Capital includes the state of ownership of the means of production by the people, the inflow of cash capital, its retention, and the ease with which it is accessible to citizens. Thus, successful government policy should ensure inflows and retention of capital. Zimbabwe has porous pockets. It does not matter how much capital it receives from the international community. The longest it can stay in the country is a few months. The porous pockets are obvious. Inflows come in; the cash goes into salaries, to commerce, or even to support the working capital needs of uncompetitive and struggling industries.

Without addressing the issue of markets, the money flows into South Africa and China to buy food, gadgets, and clothes that wear out. The uncompetitive company soon loses its working capital and goes begging again. Without addressing markets, the banks bailout proposed in 2012 serves no purpose. The same banks will lend to high risk, underperforming companies with high default rates, and the vicious cycle continues. Zimbabwe needs policies to effectively control the movement and deployment of capital.

Like the Chinese, she must specify what may be imported liberally, what will be controlled, and what needs authorisation. This way she will be able to direct her capital to productivity. She must prioritise machinery, tools, raw materials, transport and communications, and everything needed to support industry. At the same time, she must stop the import of food products that are produced locally just because they are better packaged or have a better price. Instead, she must look for further opportunities for her people to grow as producers and manufacturers.

Zimbabwe needs to better manage her export proceeds and leverage them for industrial growth. Here is a source of capital that is well within her control and influence, yet it is mismanaged. Unlike the China example, proceeds can be managed through a liberal framework, such as defining what may be imported and leaving commerce and industry to decide for itself. Anyone who needs to import what is outside the priority list would need to be licensed.

As discussed earlier, another way to direct capital into the productive sector is through the creation of profitable markets in the target sectors. Experience has shown that without regulation, capital flows into profitable areas of the economy. Zimbabwe can attract investment capital into the manufacturing sector by ensuring that the industrialist makes money in his market. This has happened in petroleum, fashion, medical, diamonds, and the gold sector, which have defied all the sanctions excuses.

Capital accumulation can be achieved through the combined policies of investment into the productive sector, exports, and import control. Zimbabwe mainly exports minerals, and world markets determine the prices. That means there are no bilateral trade obligations for consumer products in the region. What sucks the most capital from the market is one-way trade with South Africa.

The country needs to be cautious with the enticement of bilateral loans to finance infrastructure development ahead of actual wealth accumulation through productive sector investments. This concept involves advance loans with apparently generous conditions to build advanced infrastructure. They are then tied to earnings from mineral resources, the only available export commodity for the country. That means all the export earnings get mortgaged ahead of time, leaving no alternative export revenue sources to leverage for industrial growth. As stated earlier, investors do not come because of nice roads and airports. Investment follows opportunity. A population that is accumulating wealth is worth investing into, but the absence of capital will keep it poor.

Another key observation is that capital is available and can be raised, depending on the policies Zimbabwe adopts. Through the import of higher technology goods, Zimbabwe rendered her capital investment in plant and machinery redundant. Many companies, such as the National Railways of Zimbabwe and ZECO (a heavy engineering firm), are sitting on billions of dollars' worth of redundant machinery capital. These are assets with the capacity to service the engineering needs of the country, but because they have been starved of markets, they are lying idle. All the companies that closed have redundant assets that could be resuscitated. Other countries decommission plants and sell them off to lower technology producing countries.

At this rate of company closures, Zimbabwe may have to write off, in a few years, all the industrial capital she accumulated over a century. However, with a policy of import substitution and control of markets, mothballed plants can be resuscitated with little additional investment and upgrades. The pressure of technology updates will always be a factor, and there is no guarantee that an investment in new plant today will not be overtaken by new technology tomorrow. Like the arms race, a nation can end up engaged in wasteful and premature technology updates. What it means is that the third world can dictate its own technology pace, and the first world will have to wait for it, or it will be like an Olympic athlete racing with a tortoise. He will be alone in the race.

Entrepreneurship

Entrepreneurship includes the right of people to dream and engage in successful enterprise, first in their nation, and then by expanding their competitive advantage globally. This will include training programs, assistance programs, and the right to profit or reward. It is promoted by training and the availability of the factors of production. While profit motivates, it is always the reality of competition and the consequence of failure that must be considered. Opening markets must take into account that it takes a long time to build competencies, while there is always the chance that there is stronger competition out there. Since capital is scarce, there is a need to mitigate the risks of failure. However, Zimbabwe has failed to control the "bugs" that come with an open economy. Unexpected challenges, like new technology, cheaper products, bankrupt suppliers, or poor markets, are common risks leading to alarming levels of business failure.

Given the scarcity of capital, average Zimbabweans can only afford low technology and light industrial machinery. The government could focus on helping citizens access this, while opening the high-tech and capital-intensive industries to foreign investors. A practical matrix is such that when competition is high, you close markets, and when low, you open markets. That means countries must mitigate the challenges of quality and capital by protecting markets, suggesting that import substitution is the way to go.

Markets

Companies need to secure markets in their own country or abroad. While there is no control over foreign markets, it is important to know that home markets belong to domestic entrepreneurs first and foremost. For the sake of the people, Zimbabwe needs to leverage domestic markets for industrial growth. It is a strategic positioning that makes sense. Why would an embryo in an egg look for food outside when it has food within? Companies cannot go global without first feeding on home markets. They must develop core competencies in home markets before they can deploy them abroad. Train at home and fight abroad! This is the reality. Every child needs nurturing before it becomes an adult.

Therefore Zimbabwe needs to implement import substitution policies. Much as I applaud the spirit of the "Buy Zimbabwe Campaign," I am sure that these passive policies will not work. The consumer's responsibility is not to manage the economy on behalf of an aloof leadership. With few exceptions, the consumer will always choose whatever is best on the shelf. Purchasing a poor product when a better one is available will always feel like a bad decision. What is needed is a bold statement of what we must import to make things happen and then license imports that are not on the list. In other words, government will determine the supply condition of that product and authorise its import. It will also be able to make decisions based on its balance of payments position and not allow the current system of a free falling balance of payments.

The engineering industry can be resuscitated by deliberately creating markets for it. Government policy must ban the import of complete products when the country has the technology to add value to those products. Some projects have been known to import everything, when a high per centage of those components can be supplied locally.

Price considerations should not be the priority where bricks have to be imported because they are cheaper than local ones. The local cost factor is a product of the local environment, and when the environment refuses to consume its own, it dislocates itself. If we agree that the economy is a system, then it should not have a foreign body developing on it like a cancerous tumour. Just like the body is affected when a hand or ear suffers, a system is affected when one of its subsystems suffer; the system cannot disown its parts and expect to remain the same.

Markets can be created for local industry to take advantage of. Imported trucks, buses, plants, machinery, and other projects should not have 100 per cent foreign components. A policy could make it compulsory to import only bodies and chassis, allowing the local engineering industry to do the rest. Rhodesia implemented such policies with success. The demand for trucks was managed in such a way that there were industrywide benefits. The chassis and engine demanded local steel components, local suppliers supplied various other components, while the engineering industry fabricated and machined still other components. Paint suppliers, lights suppliers, and other suppliers all benefited from overall increased employment. Such a policy could convert the current \$5 Bn trade with South Africa into investment capital and markets for domestic industries. It must be noted that such policies previously gave rise to truck and bus companies, such as AVM, Deven Engineering, Trinity Engineering, and Morewear Industries, and companies like ZECO, formerly southern Africa's largest engineering company. There cannot be any expectation that anyone in Europe will purchase products from them. It has to be the local market that must buy from them. When the body refuses to use its own mouth for food intake, then there is a problem with the system.

A policy of local value addition will help create markets that can stimulate industrial growth. Many countries have already adopted policies for joint local production with suppliers. This policy helps expose local engineers and artisans to technology, builds confidence in self-reliance, and can set them up for "solo" projects in the future. Without this policy, the current crop of Zimbabwean engineers is not sufficiently challenged to stretch its technical abilities, with most engineers being reduced to fitters of foreign products.

The level of government confidence in its own engineers, scientists, and artisans is awfully low. Our government should challenge its people to take on serious engineering projects, even if they may fail. There must be acceptance that they will not get it right the first time. If they lack confidence, they can introduce experienced foreign consultants to work with them. It is thus necessary for government to deliberately allow its engineers and scientists to undertake inspiring projects. Success builds on success and can raise the level of confidence in local abilities.

Developing and nurturing supplier development programmes for local engineering and manufacturing firms can also create markets. Large companies such as the National Railways and ZESA Holdings, the nation's power company, can be required to set targets for the development of local suppliers over a number of years by providing markets for key spare parts, beginning with some of the older plants. This is the way to localise railways and power generation technology.

The overriding benefits of markets are that people can grow in experience and will eventually invent their own. The banking crisis can easily correct itself without the need for expensive and inconclusive bailouts, because performing companies repay their debts from profits. Addressing profit issues is the best way of correcting financial sector crises, because it deals with the primary cause of the problem.

The use of tariff measures to control markets works well in some countries and less well in others. Currently, the government of Zimbabwe has used this system, but the results so far have been less than impressive. In the clothing industry, corruption has been the major source of violations. Cheaper finished goods are being smuggled into the country by paying off customs officials, to the detriment of local production. It may be necessary to adopt a policy of placing the onus of proving violations on the injured party. Local companies should also have the right to require retailers to prove costs and prices, so they can be tracked back to duty violations. The injured party will thus speed up the detection, investigation, and prosecution of violators.

Zimbabwe can also leverage markets for investment. If a domestic market is sizeable enough, we can demand that foreign companies manufacture locally or else they will not be allowed to "parachute" their products into the country. They cannot have the freedom to take both profits and jobs from Zimbabwe, working from the comfort of their home bases. This kind of leverage is seen in the South African car market, which is thriving with locally manufactured foreign brands while restricting foreign imports. Through restrictive policies, South

Africa has arm-twisted foreign auto companies to invest in the country or lose access to local markets. This kind of trade-off can be replicated in television, radio, refrigeration, agricultural machinery, trucks, coaches, wagons, and other sizeable domestic markets.

Finally, as I began to understand the power of markets, I have learned to say, "Give me $10 and a market and I will be a billionaire; give me $1 Bn and no market, and I will become a pauper." However, even with the best of intentions, the failure to communicate vision leads to resistance. While a significant part of the Chinese population understood why they had to make sacrifices, even expressing public confidence in the country's vision, there were many who subscribed to a different vision. It is important for a nation's subsystems to share in one common purpose. Where there is a conflict of vision, there will be paralysis.

In China, 4 June 1989 was a decisive moment, when the protagonists had to decide, by force, in which direction the country would go. Whatever direction a country must take, it must be founded on scientific truths, for the truth will always prove itself right.

As defence attaché, I routinely met top Chinese generals. On the left, I am hosting General Xu Xin, then the deputy chief of defence staff.

Here I am accompanying Vice President Simon Vengesai Muzenda to the Great Wall of China.

In 1995, my farewell ceremony was held at Army Headquarters. I am seated second row right corner, as the commander of the army, General Constantine Chiwenga (folding legs), follows proceedings. In front of me is my former boss and chief of staff administration, Lieutenant General Amoth Chimombe.

Here I am receiving the Chinese military's August the First Medal at the end of my diplomatic service in 1992.

CHAPTER 10
Contradictions in Zimbabwe's Economy

THE ABSENCE OF A scientifically conceptualised economic thesis manifests itself in strategy and policy contradictions within the economy. The thesis should guide economic decisions. In its absence, decisions are made on an ad hoc basis without reference to the system implications. When there are contradictions, the system becomes dysfunctional. In this chapter, I want to highlight some of the systemic and strategy problems that have arisen as a result of decisions taken without considering the impact on Zimbabwe's entire system.

Policy Mismatches

Zimbabwe's banking sector grew rapidly in the years 1996–2004, with the formation of up to twelve new indigenous banks. Three of them succeeded in listing on the country's stock exchange. Many other financial institutions, such as asset management companies and real estate companies, also sprang up. However, beginning in 2004, the sector experienced performance problems due to a lack of discipline and too many speculative investments. Many asset management companies did not survive the 2004 banking crisis, while six of the original banks collapsed. In 2009, after the dollarisation of the economy, many struggled to meet the minimum capital required. They finally met the requirement after undergoing rounds of dilutions or mergers, or attracting new investors. The country has four foreign banks in Barclays, Standard Chartered PLC, Stanbic, and MBCA Bank.

The indigenous banks heeded the political call to lend to local companies after dollarisation in 2009, exposing themselves to attendant market risks, while the foreign banks maintained prudent lending criteria, brushing aside their critics. In 2012, the Ministry of Finance and Economic Planning feared that banks' non-performing loan portfolio may have been as high as 90 per cent, signaling a disaster in the financial sector. The collapse of the bank situation arises out of policy mismatches.

The government wanted banks to lend to the economy, which was the right thing to do. However, the scrapping of tariffs on basic goods and market liberalisation did not complement the lending policies of the banks. Many companies lost capital as they failed to compete. The indigenous banks that responded to government calls to lend to industry now stand accused of mismanagement, and yet they sincerely played a more progressive role than the foreign banks that withheld capital.

A Mismatch between Current Realities and Policies

Government policy also moved ahead of current realities by liberating markets when business was noncompetitive. Since achieving competitiveness is a long process while changing import regulations is a single event, the government could have mitigated the situation by protecting markets until such time as they could weather the competition.

A Mismatch between Capital and Opportunities

Everyone in Zimbabwe is crying out for cheaper capital inflows to supposedly retool industry as the final solution. Not enough of the debate is about markets. Clearly, nobody is questioning why the initial rounds of financing that took place after dollarisation in 2009 were lost. And what guarantees exist that the next round of financing will not be similarly lost? The arguments are the same in Europe, with more rounds of bailout programmes.

It is not the quantum of capital inflows that will be decisive but the quality of the markets. In fact, more capital inflows under the current conditions could become a curse. As long as the people are novices and markets are open, failure is inevitable. A 90 per cent non-performing loan book is not indicative of corruption but proof that market conditions must be addressed. When it comes to manufactured products, the first world does not reciprocate African imports of its manufactured products. Therefore, there is currently no reason to link manufacturing growth to foreign markets that do not buy African goods, except for minerals and raw materials.

A Mismatch between the Timing for Economic Liberation and Technology Upgrades

In 2009, Zimbabwe scrapped duties on basic goods to allow food imports after a political crisis saw goods disappear from shops. The strategy was meant to accommodate availability over a three-month period, until local industry was resuscitated. The policy stayed in effect for nearly three years. In 2012, the Confederation of Zimbabwe Industries called for the country's industries to be declared a national disaster. The scrapping of duties on basic goods caused the situation to worsen, since these basic products were the core technology local companies could exploit. Lowering duties had the effect of disrobing and completing the destruction of the nation's industry.

A Mismatch between Global Competitiveness and Local Industrial Performance

Zimbabwe aspires to be a global player, but a lot of preparation is needed to achieve that goal. What can she leverage to compete in the global arena? Because she imports all her machinery, she will always be second best, depending on technology that others have built. This has implications for strategic positioning; if she cannot be a technology leader, then free-trade policies work against her.

The Role of Positional Strategy

A positional strategy is what Zimbabwe is wrestling with, on both the economic and political fronts. I consider "position" to be the wisdom part of any strategy. I have often compared it to the hunter's need to hit a particular part of an animal in order to bring it down. Not every position is decisive (e.g., a leg or tail). In the military, position is called "the ground of strategic or tactical importance." It is defined as "the ground, such that when occupied, renders the enemy untenable." It's the best place to achieve victory in battle.

In the case of economic management, there are only two positions. You are either a domestic-driven economy or an export-driven economy. You have to be leaning in one direction or the other, depending on your strength. It would be folly to favour an export position if you are unable to compete in export markets. It is the same with a domestic-driven economy. The trouble with Zimbabwe is that there are problems with both positions; therefore, she is trying to make the best of both worlds. Unfortunately, you cannot do that with mutually exclusive positions. Try to create a new animal by using parts from a horse and an elephant, and the result will be ugly. A country has to decide what position to occupy. Since Zimbabwe's workers are not yet competitive, there is a strong case for a domestic-driven economy.

Zimbabwe needs to lower technology entry standards in order to accommodate her people. Lowering standards is when a nation deliberately chooses to consume its own products ahead of better international products. In the universities, you can set admission standards to straight "A pluses," but doing so means you exclude many people who do not meet that qualification. In an economy, introducing a competitive product (e.g., a Samsung phone) automatically sets a standard for your people. For anyone to succeed in that competition, they will have to equal or surpass that standard. The state has to compensate for this handicap, in much the same way that a weaker golfer can compete with a stronger one.

Lowering technology standards for a nation means either eliminating technology that is ahead of yours or taking measures that level the playing field. This may take the form of banning imports on selected industries or creating "stretch conditions" by setting import quotas to prevent marginalisation of domestic industries by superior foreign competition.

For example, in April 1981, the United States restricted imports of foreign automobiles, mainly from Japan, by the so-called "voluntary restraint agreement." She imposed quotas in response to pleas from the US auto industry that it needed time to grow strong enough to compete with imports on the free market.[37] This way, foreign and local companies can coexist, while providing much needed technology benchmarks for imitation. At the time, some US citizens felt that quotas came with a high cost, as they were forced to purchase expensive local cars. That is the time and place for systems thinking. Goals were divergent, as the consumer was only interested in price, while corporations and the state were interested in the long-term goal of maintaining local production. When there is such a conflict between goals, the state must rationalise and, as in this case, choose long-term goals over short-term pleasures.

A Mismatch between Empowerment Goals and Industrial Policy

The participation of indigenous people in shaping their economic destiny is a true mark of independence. By default of emigration, the economy became largely indigenised as more locals bought or acquired shares in various companies. This development was followed by a land redistribution programme and more recently by the indigenisation

---

37   Edward L., *The Costly Truth about Import Quotas.* February 1985, accessed 22 July 2012, http://www.heritage.org/research/reports/1985/02/the-costly-truth-about-auto-import-quotas.

law, which requires that 51 per cent of companies with a capitalisation of more than USD500,000 be localised. While physical ownership of factors of production advanced, the wholesale economic liberalisation model has done much to reverse such ownership.

The capital drought in the economy requires the return of capital from world markets, where foreigners snatch back those assets from locals at very cheap prices. It therefore becomes a contradiction to indigenisation to adopt a capital dependent growth strategy when internal resources cannot generate such capital. Without markets, there is a downward spiral in performance, leading to indebtedness and consequent loss of assets. If this policy position is maintained, one might ask what was the point of twenty years of strife in the name of indigenisation and empowerment, only to give up ground in a few years by way of foreign capital? On the other hand, a domestic-led economy and technology helps establish lasting ownership and success. Countries such as Brazil and China have their economies founded on their people's know-how, and their economies are moving in a self-sustaining upward spiral. These countries have solid internal strengths that are immune to external shocks such as sanctions and technology restrictions.

A Mismatch between Education and Skills-Development Goals

While Zimbabwe has produced highly educated people, her industrial performance does not reflect the quality of that education. The reason for that is the lack of industrial experience. Education only meets training performance standards, but experience perfects knowledge. Just as professionals like doctors, accountants, and pilots need thousands of hours of practice before they are qualified, so does any person require industrial experience before becoming operationally proficient. It is a proven fact that skills increase with frequency of use. For example, a football player out of the game for some time will lose his form. Therefore, adopting a pro-market approach provides more opportunities for secure investments, which help build up skill levels.

These contradictions point to the need to adopt a domestic-

led economy. They also point to the need for a shared vision on the positional strategy for the economy of Zimbabwe, which in this case should be a pro-market, domestic-driven economy, which leverages exports to finance domestic investments.

CHAPTER 11

Markets and Prospects for an Economic Miracle in Zimbabwe

ZIMBABWE'S OWN ECONOMIC SITUATION has already proved the importance of markets. The pockets of success in the middle of failure give clues as to what constitutes best practice. And if what has already worked in difficult times can be replicated in the whole economy, then theoretically Zimbabwe can do it. Although there has been a wholesale decline in manufacturing, there have been notable exceptions of "evergreen" companies that have performed well in the same environment. It will be a travesty of justice if we paid no attention to the factors that have defied the difficult circumstances that have affected most companies.

Thus, we must ask: Why are some manufacturing companies thriving? In his 2010 budget statement, Zimbabwe's minister of finance singled out the beverage, tobacco, and construction companies, which achieved capacity utilisation rates of above 80 per cent while most industries remained under 50 per cent.[38] Some of them have even

---

38 Zimbabwe Treasury, *National Budget Statement*, 2010, accessed 7 June 2011, http://www.zimtreasury.org/downloads/878.pdf.

invested into expansion programmes, giving the impression that others are merely complaining and covering up inefficiencies.

A desk survey of the companies revealed that they met a common criterion: a level of import entry barriers exists. They have less foreign competition or are in a monopolistic position. I can add bread bakers and telecommunications companies to the list. Along with the retail sector, they have a different set of problems. Let us take Delta, for example, the country's largest beverage manufacturing company. It has probably 98 per cent of the country's market share. They have the Coca-Cola franchise; they are part owned by the global SAB Miller Group, which has become the world's largest brewer of beer. There is negligible competition from imports. They are bankable and in a "no fail" situation.

The same factors apply for the other companies. There are no large-scale imports of beverages, bricks, cement, or tobacco. All bread and telecommunications are localised. The companies only compete against each other locally, where competition compensates each other. You can comb the industry and see that companies immune to foreign competition are doing well. These companies are courted by banks and are able to raise investment capital from anywhere in spite of the sanctions. Had these conditions applied to all other companies, they could have been equally thriving and the country could have avoided its current economic problems. What works for Delta can work for little companies as well.

Markets will always need to be addressed by the deployment of capital. If Zimbabwe is to grow, she has to find capital to deploy into various market opportunities that can be grouped and reserved for exploitation by a single company. Here is where a combination of private ingenuity and government prudence will pay off. The private sector can complement the government by sourcing private capital as long as opportunities are good. Let us learn from the realities of market responsiveness that have occurred in the past as models to follow in the manufacturing sector.

In 2005, the nation ran out of fuel. The National Oil Company of Zimbabwe, the state energy-procuring company, ran out of foreign currency to procure fuel. The country's treasury ran dry while foreign oil companies such as BP, Caltex (Chevron), Engen, and Total were reluctant to risk their foreign currency in a market that sold the product in a highly inflationary currency. This led to an energy crisis, with people spending days on fuel queues and families even taking turns sleeping on the queue. The government took a policy decision to allow anybody with money to import and sell their own fuel. The policy became a miracle solution. Fuel capital became available, as if someone had summoned it from all the caves and creeks where it had been hiding. Within a matter of weeks, the country was awash with fuel. Market forces had corrected the situation. What solved the problem was the profit motive. The fact that capital follows profit can be traced at various periods of the economic decline.

Popular domestic investment destinations that sprang up include start-ups in hospitals and drug distribution, banking, asset management, fashion, supermarkets, fuel, and, more recently, auto sales. Our people seem to ask, "Where is the money being made these days?" And when they learn, they invest. And they all seem to follow each other in a "me too" mentality. When tobacco growing proved to be a profitable business, production jumped to 120 million kg in 2010, having previously averaged 70 million kg during the inflationary Zimbabwe dollar era. This illustrates that, given markets, the Zimbabwean economy can take off rapidly without the overstated need for foreign investment.

As a result of this herd mentality, we see a cycle of opportunity, investment response, attractive profit taking, diminishing profits, and ultimately disinvestment or stability. These investment waves can be replicated in manufacturing too. All the country needs is a magnet of profitability conditions, and the rest of the factors will take care of themselves. The key is to ride on this profit motive and direct this capital potential into manufacturing. To do this, the country needs to corner the markets for its people by controlling imports where there is a local manufacturing capability. Government should ensure that no local manufacturer loses market share to a foreign company.

Just make sure the industrialist is the guy who drives the latest car in town and you will see the wave of "me toos" following. With her level of education and entrepreneurship, Zimbabwe is ripe for an economic miracle. To illustrate the effect of our misguided economic policies, there are no industrialists in the nation. They are not noticeable because of their poverty. There is no wealth creation in the nation. We have business leaders who, since independence, specialised in the acquisition of existing companies only. With few exceptions, new ventures are rare.

While we are strong in commercial activities, the nation has really no teeth.

A nation whose economy is skewed this way is like an army that has logistical services without fighting troops. Industry is the equivalent of real fighting troops, while commerce plays a support and facilitation role. I believe that this policy could be directed to all the low hanging technology areas, such as food processing, plastics engineering, building materials, steel fabrication, agricultural chemicals, and construction. In addition, the country could adopt a technology-nurturing scheme where investment in new technology areas could be supported through monitoring and correcting the competitive environment in favour of the local company.

Markets are the fertile ground in which companies grow. Unfortunately, those companies that are having it easy mislead politicians by advocating market liberalisation, not on the basis of broad-based rationality, but because of self-interest and self-advantage. Naturally, politicians do not listen to perceived failures. Proper economic policy is rarely a scientific process but rather an influence game. Those who are lucky to be successful get the political voice, but politicians are unaware that they are only successful because they are in the right markets at the right time or have had the opportunity to pounce on lucrative business assets.

A few exceptions exist, but there is no single business leader who is far superior to the others. If placed in another industry, he would struggle just as the others do. Yes, mismanagement does exist in some cases, but this is compensated for by the fact that local competition kills mismanaged companies and empowers the well-managed ones. This is no loss to the country, as it is merely the principle of displacement within common borders; in contrast, foreign imports destroy a country's industry.

Superiority of business leadership depends on the quality of what you leverage. Zimbabwe has provided all the lessons. We have seen business gurus rise and fall depending on the season and the quality of the opportunity. And without mentioning names, the nation has read about the rough and tumble taking place. What about the weak millions who are in the streets? There is a saying in the military, "The army marches at the pace of the slowest man." You may be a genius, but victory for the nation is only arrived at when the slowest man has occupied his ground.

Therefore, let us recognise the millions of the voiceless would-be entrepreneurs who would like to realise their dreams. Let us think of the few unknown but core industrialists at heart, who have hung in there against the odds. Let them be rewarded, for they will create jobs and produce wealth for the nation. Let us think of a grandmother who could smile if she did not lose the market for her tomatoes because someone is importing them.

There are many who have dared to invest their hard-earned savings but soon closed their business because superior foreign products were allowed into the market, flushing their dreams, sweat, and energy down the drain. Not only have they lost their savings, but they immediately became the banker's number one enemy. More recently, in 2012, it hit home to the captains of industry when the Confederation of Zimbabwe Industries called for the industrial decline to be declared a national disaster.

Our response to that should be an active and aggressive pro-markets strategy.

CHAPTER 12
Zimbabwe in Global Competition: Free Trade or Protectionism?

Is ZIMBABWE READY TO be a global market player? Sadly, it is still only a wish. Reality has proved us wrong. Prior to 1993, before South Africa joined the Southern African Development Coordinating Conference (SADCC), Zimbabwe was the boastful big fish in the southern African economic pond. She was arrogant to the point of bemoaning the absence of South Africa in the pond. Politicians believed we could beat South Africa in their own backyard.

Although I appreciate Zimbabwe's never dying optimism, I must note that it has also become a handicap, a kind of morphine that dulls the pain necessary for alternative solutions. South Africa proved that a superior force overruns the weaker one. No sooner had she been admitted to the new economic block, than she began running a trade surplus of billions of rand over Zimbabwe.

Zimbabwe quickly moved from a favourable balance of trade position to negative at the onset of liberation. In 1988, Zimbabwe's GDP was USD4.6 Bn. Imports registered were USD1.1 Bn against exports of USD1.6 Bn, with a trade surplus of USD0.5 Bn.[39] The trade deficit continued to rise annually. In 2011 trade with South Africa accounted for 64.5 per cent of the total import bill of USD8.6 Bn, against exports of USD3.5 Bn, displaying an ever-widening trade gap. South Africa enjoyed the largest share of imports into the country by any individual country, while Kuwait comes a distant second at 10.8 per cent, with the others being China (4.5 per cent); Zambia (2.5 per cent); Mozambique (1.9 per cent); and the rest of the world with an insignificant 15.4 per cent.

Figure 5: Zimbabwe's Imports by Country, 2011

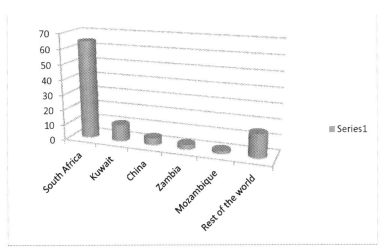

Source: Zimstats[40]

The trade deficit in 2011 has widened to $5 Bn, a figure that is more than the export value of $3.5 Bn, demonstrating how much the country has sank. This deficit represents capital that could have been saved and sunk into production, wealth, and employment creation

39   Gregory Copley, *Defence and Foreign Affairs Handbook, 1990–1991* (International Media Corporation, 1989).

40   Zimstat, 2012, http://www.zimstat.co.zw/dmdocuments/Trade/ Bulletin/Summary.pdf.

had the country followed the China model of focusing on productive consumption.

The nature and type of Zimbabwe's imports can give insight into possible savings and growth areas, had the country been oriented towards a pro-markets and pro-domestic industry strategy.

Zimbabwe's 2011 Imports by Category

PRODUCT DESCRIPTION	US$ (Bns)	% Imports
Food and Beverages	0.9	10
Raw Materials	3.9	45
Fuels and Lubes	0.1	1
Machinery and Tools	0.9	11
Transport and Passenger Vehicles	1.2	14
Consumer Goods	0.5	5
Others Not Classified	1.2	14
TOTALS	8.5	100%

Source: Zimstats[41]

The analysis of the import bill shows that Zimbabwe is not really a global player in trade. South Africa is the dominant trade partner, and dealing with that trade relationship can change the fortunes of the nation. It is also to be noted that there is no direct trade with the United States and other nations. The United States exports mostly information technology products that come indirectly through South Africa's re-export business.

What could be the impact of protectionism in Zimbabwe? For all it matters, protection would not directly hurt South Africa, as she is re-

---

41   Zimstat, 2012, http://www.zimstat.co.zw/dmdocuments/Trade/ Bulletin/Summary.pdf.

exporting mostly finished products from other parts of the world. Apart from the conflict with the principle of free trade, the United States and other nations will not be hurt by protectionism, as their direct trade with Zimbabwe is minuscule. However, the benefits of savings in low technology products will still accrue to high tech industries of the United States, as savings will now be applied to such acquisitions as passenger aircraft, transport, and communications, which are currently not affordable since the national airline Air Zimbabwe is now grounded.

Opportunities Inherent in the Import Pattern

Discussion earlier had focused on some of the policies that could be activated to help Zimbabwe out of its current crisis. Some of the policies mentioned included import restrictions, such as a ban on foodstuffs locally produced, and promoting the importation of semi-finished vehicles and products. An analysis of the breakdown of imports reveals some opportunities to close the import gap, to raise capital, and to channel it back into the productive sector.

Zimbabwe Imports by Category and Analysis of Potential

Product Description	US$ (Bns)	% Imports	Potential Savings
Food and Beverages	0.9	10	0.6
Primary Raw Materials	0.3	3	
Processed Raw Materials	3.6	42	1.8
Fuels and Lubes	0.1	1	
Machinery and Tools	0.9	11	
Noncommercial Transport	0.5	6	0.2
Commercial Transport	0.5	6	
Parts and Accessories	0.1	2	
Consumer Goods	0.5	5	
Others Not Classified	1.2	14	0.6
Totals	8.5	100%	3.2

Source: Zimstats

An expenditure of $1 Bn in food and beverages is something that can be avoided, given that Zimbabwe is a country with idle capital, plants, and machinery that once produced these products. Such consumption adversely affects local wines, spirits, flour, fruit, vegetables, and vegetable fats. There is real potential to knock down $600 million in expenditures, while resuscitating mothballed industries.

Processed raw materials represent an investment opportunity for foreign and domestic companies. These raw materials must be analysed and investment made into those specific areas. An investor with resources can be guaranteed the market segment. The country's grain and flourmills are lying idle because private interests have been allowed to import cheaper flour from Turkey. The country must import wheat and let the local mills process it into flour.

Noncommercial transport represents small passenger vehicles.

Zimbabwe imports mostly Japanese used cars, which are cheaper. However, the public has resorted to these due to poor investment in public transport. The corresponding challenge has been traffic congestion on an already poor infrastructure. In 2011 the total import bill for used vehicles exceeded $1 Bn. This is hardly a good story for a country that cannot raise even $100 m from IMF and the World Bank. There are opportunities to leverage this by either investing more into public transport or attracting another auto manufacturing company to produce vehicles locally.

There should not be any restrictions on commercial transport and vehicles, as these are the payloads needed to accelerate growth. However, commercial transport importation can be leveraged to create employment and improve local skills by importing semi-finished vehicles and equipment where possible. Certainly, there are engineering companies to build bus and truck bodies. Only 50 per cent of the cost is imported. This could see the country saving or retaining $250 m of the costs, while at the same time creating downstream jobs.

Consumer goods represent 5 per cent of the import bill. As I see it, this is an insignificant number given the social cost of restricting them. It would be prudent for the government to allow this to remain an open area. However, the state could put this on the monitoring list, especially where there is need to put a cap on expenditures.

Various other imports were not classified. These amounted to USD1.2 Bn or 14 per cent of the import bill of USD8.5 Bn. Their cost to the nation can also be evaluated. There are far too many nonproductive assets, such as telecommunications infrastructure that is being duplicated by companies instead of sharing. Mobile companies such as Econet Wireless, Telecel, Net One, and Africom are each stepping on each other to mount communications towers on the same spot and digging up redundant trenches for optic fibre.

The question remains, "What is the cost of free competition?" In 2012 Econet Wireless completed a $300 m capital raising exercise to increase infrastructure. Each of the four nonproductive telecommunications companies will have to do the same, costing the country $1.2 Bn in the next two years. These companies do not export anything and will crowd out much needed capital from the productive sector. The state must either prescribe compulsory sharing or reduce the number of players through mergers to prevent waste through duplication of infrastructure. The current situation threatens to mortgage the future of the country and take substantial capital away from the productive sector with consequent long-term commitments in debt amortization.

Zimbabwe Not a Global Competitor

The trade numbers make it clear that Zimbabwe is not a global state, and its trade is largely bilateral. It does not yet have the competencies to compete in the world. Within the region, it does not even have one consumer brand that has entered the South African market. If she is going to build her own brands, she must start from home.

Zimbabwe must therefore withdraw from this global herd mentality and retreat into its realities to enable the state to make corporate choices on sourcing from global markets. Parasitic organisations like Pick 'n Pay must only be used as demo institutions for our people to imitate. They should not be allowed to grow chains around the country as long as they are importing and promoting South African products at the expense of local companies. Local supermarket chains must be compelled to act responsibly by giving shelf space to local companies. The Pick 'n Pay model is synonymous with economic terrorism, as the company becomes a logistics base for South African operations.

While Zimbabwe's withdrawal from world trade is inconsequential to the rest of the world, it will be felt in South Africa. Because of the symbiotic relationship with South Africa, there will always be ways of compensating South Africa through directed trade or most favoured nation status for most of the key industrial machinery and raw materials. An economically growing Zimbabwe will be good for the world. The strategy is not a withdrawal from trade, rather a redeployment of trade priorities, shifting the focus from frivolous basics to larger, high technology products. This position will actually increase trade with the United States, China, and other countries that are at the technological high end. Savings from the technology low end will be deployed to the purchase of passenger aircraft, high tech machinery, and infrastructure.

The "locust" approach to trade, which strips every green leaf from treetops to the ground, is not acceptable. It marginalises, disempowers, and impoverishes its victims. There will be nothing left for the goats and cattle to feed on. For example, China's range of technology is so broad that without state intervention, no one can compete with her products. At the same time, what I call the "giraffe" position is more like the US technology position, which is at the high end and consequently does not compete with the lower market opportunities of weaker economies.

Free Trade versus Protectionism

There is a compelling need to protect Zimbabwe's industry, but perhaps these needs will apply to all nations that are having economic difficulties due to competitive pressures. It is clear that more research alone will not restore the situation; only by correcting markets can we bring economies back into balance. For this reason, discussion of free trade versus protectionism takes centre stage. My observation is that there are so many good arguments on both sides that the debate has become polarised. However, I want to add what I think is a new dimension to the debate.

Free Trade

If a nation is technologically superior, it will benefit from free trade. The weaker nations will, at the same time, see it as a disadvantage. The race has to be handicapped for weaker nations if they are to have a chance of winning. As the policy now stands, the strong are guaranteed to win. With only thirty-two years of independence and no managerial and manufacturing experience, what can Zimbabweans do to compete against advanced cultures with centuries of industrial experience? These are the crucial issues to be considered.

Free trade helps accelerate creativity and technology, but without controls it ends up hurting world trade. It currently represents the one-sided freedom to kill the competition. But freedom itself has another side: the freedom to compete or not to compete. Secondly, free trade removes the capacity of a state to direct central strategy, which is a violation of the scientific principles of management, resulting in the predetermined outcome of a race between unequal nations.

Even with such competition, there is no finish line (i.e., a red line determining where and when to stop, especially as fiscal measures fail to remedy runaway trade deficits). Thank God for the balance of nature that is coming to the rescue as a product of the current financial crisis.

Protectionism

It follows that protectionism is an antithesis to a stronger nation. It harms that nation's imperial ambitions. It harms nations with appetites beyond their own borders. I am convinced that trade will always be good. In a humane world, it can promote the mutual growth of both parties, with each fertilising the other with its unique gifts. Freedom should really come from a sense of "not being or not feeling compelled."

Each nation should choose to compete or not to compete. If other states are restricting exports for strategic reasons, does it not follow that it can also restrict imports? Therefore, protectionism should be a strategic option for an autonomous state. It gives back rights to a state to protect its people from the fate of irrational and fatal competition.

Consumer choices that are violated by protectionism can only be enjoyed when the national environment has been corrected. The scientific truth is that the part is subordinate to the whole. Just as a tyre is customised to a type of car, consumer choices should be customised to the national design. Arguments about consumer rights are frivolous, especially where they violate scientific principles of management.

The Chinese were particularly good at subordinating individualism to collectivism in a systemic way. Whenever I visited a Chinese province, a governor's briefing always started with a description of the higher national plan before describing their role in it. The armed forces also use this practice to align individual goals with higher goals. When issuing operational orders and plans, they always start with a higher level plan and then go on to describe the details of their plan. A state whose plans are designed and coordinated to all the entities involved will be strong. Even soccer teams plot a game plan; the players know their roles, from goalkeeper, to defenders, to midfielders, to strikers. They always play to a higher purpose before playing for themselves.

These principles are violated when nations adopt wholesale

liberalisation. Do corporate executives understand the national economic plan? Can they honestly see themselves contributing to it in a positive way when scoring own goals through irresponsible imports?

To sum up this part, we see that free trade and protectionism are mutually exclusive ideas. It is impossible to be agreeable outside a shared destiny and shared benefits. They describe the saying, "One man's meat is another man's poison." This problem is caused by an attempt to take benefits for some while rejecting the negative consequences for all. The principle of "common market borders, uncommon political borders" does not work. It is like a neighbour jumping over the wall to rob someone and then going back to feed his family only.

The Global Solution

The principle of free markets outside political integration is not working. Nations will increasingly demand control of their own destinies. We will see more nations pulling out of common markets that disadvantage them. The emerging solutions lie in either of the following approaches.

One approach is called Common Market Borders, Common Political Borders (CMB-CPB). This approach entails the total liberation of markets under one politically integrated trading block. In this block, citizens share the risks and profits of free trade through a central government. A good example is the United States, where the state allows free interstate trade and mitigates risks through mutual responsibility for social, economic, and other challenges.

The alternative is the "super free-market" proposal of the Uncommon Market Borders, Uncommon Political Borders (UMB-UPB) approach. This is where markets are grouped under a political state that rationalises damage from competition. This means that Zimbabwe (or any independent state) should have the right to organise its macro- and microeconomics to compete within and outside its political borders. It will be a competition of states, not companies, with states determining trade choices. A state can use this freedom to formulate a game plan that will help it industrialise.

CHAPTER 13

Deploying the Factors

RESEARCH HAS SHOWN THAT wherever the five factors of production have been synchronised, success has resulted. Wherever one or more of them has been missing, failure has been the outcome. Markets, the predominant factor, are associated with social, economic, and political stability. There is ample evidence of the correlation between the provision of markets and the rapid growth of whole industries in Zimbabwe.

Figure 6: The Combination Key for a
Successful Manufacturing Environment

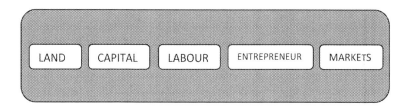

A few examples will help drive the point home. The tobacco industry had collapsed in the first few years since land redistribution. On each of the occasions it failed, it was due to the lack of implements or inputs that came late (capital), untrained farmers (labour and entrepreneurship), or inappropriate prices (poor markets due to the inflation-prone Zimbabwe dollar era). When the economy was dollarised, farmers received good value (markets), leading to a jump in production from 70 million kg to 120 million kg of tobacco in one year.

Markets again resulted in the success of the local music industry through the "75 per cent local content" policy. The policy reversed the foreign dominated music industry by stipulating mandatory air play of 75 per cent local music on radio and television. As more play time was given to native musicians, local artists mushroomed, and the quality of the music rapidly improved.

The deployment of the factors of production activates the working of the "Five *I*s," a learning and continuous improvement process that is necessary for industrialisation based on internal strengths. Nations that have industrialised successfully have beaten the same familiar path, beginning with 1) poor imitations, like a child imitating its mother, 2) improvement, and then 3) improvisation as creativity starts building up, followed by 4) innovation, culminating in the 5) invention stage.[42]

This was the Japanese model, according to Singaporean researchers, and we see the same with China and India. In technological development, there are no quantum leaps. Technology leaders create a monopoly over markets and are thus able to develop under a continuous improvement mode where they make mistakes without someone overtaking them.

The "Five *I*s" process view of industrial development can be replicated in Zimbabwe. For example, over the past five years, the country has imported thousands of tractors from Western manufacturers such as John Deere, Massey Fergusson, New Holland, Case, Landini, and Renault, to little known Eastern brands from China, India, Iran, and South Korea. In 2011, the first tractor manufacturing joint venture

---

42   Chow-Hou Wee, Khai Sheang Lee, and Bambang Walujo Hidajat, *Sun Tzu, War and Management: Application to Strategic Management and Thinking* (Addison-Wesley, 1996).

(JV) was established with an Iranian company. This could be taken as entry-level technology, as it is not the best tractor in the world, yet it has all the utility value of a modern tractor. Given a choice between it and John Deere, the Iranian tractor would have no chance. But import restrictions can help develop the brand into an international brand over time, through the continuous improvement process.

The spin-off benefits are invaluable. The technology mastered from component production can then be applied not only to tractors, but also to a variety of related products and applications, giving rise to a number of related industries and products. With a hypothetical market of five thousand tractor units per year, the JV can sell USD100 million's worth of tractors per year. However, because of a split market share across ten brands in the industry, its annual sales can only be USD10 million, or five hundred units. This is the effect of free trade in a situation where your own company has no global reach to compensate for a reduced home market. The investment may actually be lost as the JV struggles to make a profit.

The history of the automobile industry shows a clear and continuous improvement path from the earlier models. If nobody bought those successive models, then we would never have gotten to where we are today. As technology laggards, we can create our own technology leadership by having our own technology entry point, while restricting the entry of superior products that substitute local ones. Interestingly, nature behaves much the same. When you plant a crop under a big tree, it dies because the big tree takes the sunshine away. If you want the crop to grow, you must cut the big tree.

The Chinese Air Force did just that. Realising that it was behind in fighter aircraft technology, it made a technology leap by acquiring the Soviet Sukhoi SU27 squadron and used that technology platform to build its own variants of fighter aircraft with successive technology upgrades. Meanwhile, the Chinese Air Force appeared to be oblivious of the arms race and was comfortable with having its new but below-par aircraft run its full life cycle. It would not be drawn into a product race because it was more interested in mastering technology than in the state-of-the-art products themselves. In this way, China quickly caught up with the superpowers in fighter aircraft technology.

The lesson is if you want to grow your own industries, you have to find a way for people to buy and use their own products. The choice

Zimbabwe has is simple: she either gobbles up imports and face her own death, or refrains and survive. It is a proven reality that short-term goals have long-term consequences. The control of imports and the creation of local markets for domestic companies may appear to curtail consumer choice, but it is, in the long term, the only guarantee of consumer choice, as the Chinese model has proved.

Once a government has provided the five factors of production, the continuous improvement model kicks in automatically, provided the system retains a measure of openness so that the external environment influences the internal environment. Total isolation, such as that experienced by China from 1950 to 1979, is retrogressive, as its citizens were left behind while the world marched on.

However, in this ideal environment, government ceases to be important, as the spotlight shifts to business performance. Because of economic hardships today, governments are on the lips of people daily. Consequently, there should be agreement that the five factors are what constitute the vital national interests of any nation. Once agreed, as in the American democracy, it will not matter which political party comes to power, since the object of political association will no longer be a contest over ideology and direction, but on the management of agreed national interests. Since the five factors are the backbone of the life and economy of the people, they should form part of Zimbabwe's vital national interests.

The absence of a consensus on national interests is an obstacle to Zimbabwe's fledgling democracy. There are sharp differences over national strategic interests and their ownership, with one side believing possession and ownership by the people is not the issue, but rather trading them for short term bread-and-butter issues is. While there are passionate arguments on both sides, I am convinced that the five factors of production are non-negotiable for a nation that seeks to determine its own destiny. Hence, it is the people themselves who must come to understand their non-negotiable interests and elect politicians based on their ability to strengthen the nation's strategic interests. History has constantly showed that land, people, capital, entrepreneurship, and markets are well worth fighting for.

CHAPTER 14

Democracy or National Interests?

ZIMBABWE BECAME A DEMOCRACY after the liberation war forced Ian Smith's Rhodesian government to accept an inclusive popular democracy that catapulted President Mugabe to power in 1980. Since then, democratic elections have been held every five years, with some of the results being contested. There is contention over the existence of democracy in Zimbabwe, but the issues under debate straddle across national interests and destiny. There are disagreements over the quality of democracy, land redistribution, and indigenisation.

The nation's understanding of democracy is important. While Zimbabweans are fighting over the meaning of democracy, it would appear that other nations have long moved past the idealism of democracy to self-interest. We need to rethink the doctrine that democracy is a panacea for our problems. The United States has already proved that she is not preoccupied with guarding democracy per se, as if it were an end in itself. Instead, she has used democracy to guard something else that matters more to it: US interests.

These are those economic and security interests that enhance the quality of American lives. Anyone who is perceived to act against these interests has been regarded as an enemy. The United States has demonstrated time after time that she will go to bed with dictators if they can guard her interests, and she will effect "regime change" on democracies that fail to protect her interests. We can scan the globe and see the US's flirtations with authoritarian regimes, such as that of Mobuto Seseko of the Democratic Republic of Congo, apartheid South Africa, the Emirates, Kuwaitis, Saudis, Bahrainis, and, until recently, Pakistanis and Egyptians. At the same time, she has shown hostility towards other authoritarian regimes such as Syria, Libya, and democratic Iran, only for resisting US interests. If we place a democracy template over the world, it would not pass as the US objective for the world. Yet if we apply a "national interests" template, it is 100 per cent correct that the United States guards her interests wherever they are. Democracy is only a means to an end.

Through a dictatorship, China has successfully guarded her treasure to ensure the progress of her people. Here is a dictatorship that has delivered, and no one dares talk about it. I am not denigrating democracy, because I think Zimbabwe needs democracy as a tool to replace leaders. But we must guard against its abuse by outside powers that seek to usurp the vital national interests of our people. In our case, we must see beyond democracy if we are going to make correct judgements.

Zimbabwe's democracy can be strengthened through a national consensus about what constitutes national interests based on the five factors of production. The state's institutions must then defend these interests. Secondly, Zimbabwe must then have a transparent and democratic process for electing a government whose mandate is to protect the agreed interests. Such a government must be led by a strong presidency with a limited term of office. Creating weak leadership or institutions that result in operational stalemates for elected executives is detrimental to progress. The systems approach discussed earlier emphasises the need for central leadership and purpose. The economy will require effective direction and execution from the centre if there is to be progress. The defined national interests will provide a framework to limit the potential excesses of the executive. The executive's mandate is to manage and enhance the quality of the national interests, and, in this way, it will not be difficult to see which executive is getting out of line.

The lesson we must take from this is that democracy is a system that allows a nation to change its leaders. As servants of the people, leaders must guard the nation's heritage. In the United States, heritage is equated with interests she will shed blood for. Zimbabweans appear to make light work of their heritage. They have not learned from their role model (the United States) that national interests are vital. Consequently, they seem to be more concerned with democracy than with what democracy stands to keep or give away.

I want to conclude by saying that, whatever political party or charismatic person arrives in our future, whatever system of governance becomes fashionable, the key is to keep our eyes on the treasure of the five factors of production. These are national interests, because they promote the economic well-being of all the people. Therefore, systems of government should always be subordinate to the overall national interests.

CHAPTER 15

The New World Economic and Social Order

THE NEW WORLD ORDER is a much-debated topic. It has been understood to mean that a world government will emerge that is led by civilised Western capitalism and orchestrated by powerful secret societies. This dictatorial government will monopolise wisdom to determine the fate of nations from a powerful centre. For a time, the rise of the US and Western powers has almost made this a possibility. Since, at present, this dominance is in check, new meanings have to be discerned from this. The rise of China and, more recently, India necessitates a review of long held views regarding the powers that will impose this new world order. Dr Robert Hsu, editor of *China Strategy* and a Chinese American, published the following startling revelations about rising Chinese power:[43]

> The center of all commerce and wealth will shift from the U.S. economy and U.S. companies to the Chinese economy and Chinese companies, as they will ultimately be the biggest profit

---

43 Robert Hsu, "Secret IMF Report Reveals Our Next 10 Bagger," *The China Strategy*, 23 May 2011.

takers of this new economic order. To think that just 10 years ago the U.S. economy was three times the size of China's! Now, in just five short years, their economy will be bigger than ours, not only for the rest of our investing lives, but also for that of every generation of Americans to come.

You won't read one word on how the Chinese economy will ultimately overtake the U.S. economy, and how mutual fund insiders and institutional investors are buying up China's top companies for pennies on the dollar.

This is why Warren Buffett dropped $200 million on a Chinese car company in an unstable nation filled with liars and thieves.

This is why McDonald's is opening a new store every three days.

This is why Amazon.com opened nine new warehouses this year.

This is why Apple is manufacturing their iPhone, iPod, iMacs, and iPads there–all in anticipation of the huge profit wave that will come from new China sales.

The REAL CHINA that is creating thousands of new millionaires every day.

The REAL CHINA that needs to build 11 New York–sized cities by 2030 to handle the rising population.

The REAL CHINA that is the world leader in wind energy, auto production, and energy usage.

The REAL CHINA that has the fastest bullet train, the first mass-produced plug-in hybrid, and now the world's fastest supercomputer.

The REAL CHINA that will surpass the U.S. economy in the next five years and change the investing landscape forever.

What we can read from Dr Hsu's summary is that the United States, and the West in general, may not impede China's growth by more marketing, training and research, and austerity measures, including all the business climate politics they have at their disposal, which have thus far characterised economic reforms. China is unstoppable, but only education and an understanding of the limits of irresponsible exploitation will create a more equitable development environment through negotiation of economic space. This defines the future into which we are heading.

At this breakneck speed, the Chinese economy will swallow every nation. China may even impoverish others if she continues along the path of irresponsible capitalism (i.e., winner take all). What is important to observe is that, as long as she operates according to the laws and principles of capitalism, she will eventually meet the US economic fate. The crisis of capitalism lies in its refusal to share wealth accumulated by others (i.e., the 1 per cent of wealthy billionaires who keep all the wealth to themselves, while existing alongside the 99 per cent of less fortunate people).

The current economic situation, emerging out of increasing competition from other nations, implies that the concept of interdependency has to be acknowledged. China cannot produce everything for the world. She must allow other countries a role in contributing to the world economy. For as long as she overly dominates markets, China will increasingly face American wrath and will need to temper her successes.

If a country cannot contribute to the global economic system, it ceases to be part of the world trading system, which, in turn, harms world trade. This interdependency will cause some of the economic mountains in China, the United States, Japan, and the EU to melt down. These countries will maintain technology leadership in some core industries, while giving up market territory to others. In the process, some of their companies will close down while new opportunities will open up for other nations.

It is still possible that the likes of Boeing and Microsoft will remain vehicles for elevating the economic fortunes of the United States, while the country performs poorly in other sectors. If this happens, the challenge will be in distributing the wealth generated by a few large, highly performing industries, while others lick their wounds. This is the problem the United States faces today, and it is only the beginning, as evidenced by the Occupy Wall Street movement. If the wealth distribution challenge cannot be resolved, capitalism will be overthrown by its own masses.

This movement will continue to grow for as long as the United States loses markets under free-trade policies and the gap between rich and poor widens. In contrast, cooperation in trade will look at levelling the inequalities, giving each nation a piece of the pie and ensuring that each nation can grow economically. The world is a system, and a system is disabled when a part is removed from it; the entire world suffers when a part of it suffers.

It appears that globalisation, and its effects on weaker nations, is self-correcting to the centre. Just as the Earth and all planets are in perfect balance, the world economy will eventually reach equilibrium. Capitalism was called to rethink its premise when, as soon as it had celebrated its victory over communism, it found itself in a crisis. Equality is being forced upon the world by the balance of nature. The Bible says, "Every valley shall be exalted and every mountain and hill brought low; the crooked places shall be made straight and the rough places smooth."[44] Nature will ultimately raise the valleys and lower the mountains, but these changes will be less painful if the world manages them voluntarily. Locally, weaker nations can raise the valleys and lower the mountains when out of necessity they begin to protect their markets. This is not a matter of choice; the negative effects of globalisation compel them to do so. The outcome, which is an economic slowdown for the stronger economies and rapid growth for the weaker ones, is very much a matter of fait accompli. These adjustments will result in the equality of nations.

The forces of levelling are already in motion. On 30 March 2012, China issued the following statement, headlined "China imports present huge opportunity for world":[45]

> Beijing: Measures to promote balanced trade currently being deliberated by the Chinese authorities may create significant opportunities for other countries if implemented. The State Council, or China's cabinet, said in a statement released last Friday [30 March 2012] after an executive meeting that China is considering a number of policies to boost the country's imports and improve its trade balance. The country will adopt measures to adjust import tariffs and facilitate fund-raising and customs clearances for importing

44 John C. Maxwell, "Isaiah 40:4," in *The Maxwell Leadership Bible*, New Kings James Version (Nashville: Thomas Nelson Publishers, 1982) 851.
45 Staff Reporter, "China Imports Present Huge Opportunity for World," *The Zimbabwe Herald*, 4 April 2012, 8.

enterprises, according to the statement. China will cut import duties on some energy and raw material products, as well as several high-tech goods, by implementing temporary tariff rates, the statement said. Deputy Minister of Commerce Zhong Shan said the ministry will soon introduce guidelines for boosting imports and promoting trade balance. "I'd like to send a clear signal that China's imports will provide huge business opportunities for other countries," Zhong said.[46]

This is arguably the first time a nation voluntarily sought to accommodate other nations by encouraging imports. Traditionally such measures are done as part of aid to weaker nations. The significance is that China appears to be clear on its global role and appears to understand how its industrial power can damage world trade with consequent harm to itself. However, even with this apparent noble gesture, the type of imports show that China's imports remain strategically designed to strengthen her global economic leadership. With these rare voluntary measures, there is hope for managed change into this new world.

---

46 Xinhua News, "China Imports Present Huge Opportunity for the World," *Xinhuanet*, 30 March 2012, accessed 30 July 2012, http://news.xinhuanet.com/english/china/2012-03/31/c_131501594.htm.

CHAPTER 16
Conclusion

THE SECRET TO THE success of "rabble" economies lies in the climate created by the supply condition of all five factors of production. In essence, a rabble economy is one that has an appearance of chaos at the surface but is being guided by the underlying five factors of production, which fuel the emergence of a superior economy. Any country that successfully addresses all factors of production will experience economic success. The emerging economies provided and nurtured the existence of all factors of production over a long period of time.

The principle of free markets is a doctrine of the strong; it is reached when industrial output surpasses domestic consumption. A weaker economy must take this into account when entering bilateral and multilateral free-trade agreements.

A country's trade policy evolves over time in relation to the growing industrial strength or weaknesses of its economy. The best time to enter a free-trade agreement is when you are able to compete.

In Zimbabwe's history, the years of Rhodesian sanctions from 1965 to 1979 saw the nation rapidly industrialise because all five factors of production were present in the economy. It failed to industrialise in subsequent years because the five factors of production had been disrupted by migration, ESAP, and smart sanctions.

In 1992, Zimbabwe misdiagnosed the cause of economic stagnation and embraced ESAP, which disrupted markets for domestic industries, leading to severe economic, social, and political problems.

At the global level, the rise of Asia's industrial competitiveness at the expense of Western dominance has put the reality of global free-market policies in check, as the hunter has become the hunted.

As global markets will only expand when each country can increase its wealth, there is a growing dependence on the Commonwealth of Nations for global trade to continue. Consequently, the economic success of all nations shall be of interest to all.

Market cooperation, rather than increased protectionism, will become the only way to resolve trade disputes harmoniously.

Markets must be recognised as the fifth factor of production because of their huge influence on economic success.

Zimbabwe's vital national interests must include all the factors of production, as they are essential to a happy and prosperous nation.

Democracy itself is not an end but a system of selecting leadership that must look after the national interests of the country. A nation must set its sights not only on democracy, but also on those factors of production democracy stands to preserve.

An industronometer is a useful tool for assessing the health of an economy by measuring the supply conditions of the factors of production.

The rabble economy's miracle lies in experimentation and continuous improvement in a risk free economic environment. Through these laboratory conditions, the people can master technology to catch up with the rest of the world.

Involvement of a critical mass of the population in economic activity is the key to gaining mastery of technology. The people will need access to and ownership of the means of production in order to be involved in progressive experimentation.

Land reform and indigenisation of the economy are a necessary part of ownership of the means of production, so that productive experimentation leading to mastery can occur.

An industrial *evolution* (not revolution) can take place when leaders are patient with the people, allowing the process of imitation, improvement, improvisation, innovation, and invention to occur in an economy. The failure to appreciate this gradual process view can lead to wasteful changes in developmental plans.

A genuine democracy can emerge when the people's loyalty shifts to the idealism of national interests in the five factors of production, away from party and personality politics. This way they can guard their destiny by measuring political parties on the basis of their ability to preserve the five factors of production.

CHAPTER 17

The Blueprint

Application of the Rabble Lessons

THE CENTRAL THESIS OF this book points to the dangers any country faces when it fails to follow a policy of strategic positioning within the world economic system. The national economies that are performing poorly have lost their system or business model, in terms of purpose, design, and implementation. They have lost sight of whose interests must be served by an economy. They have lost sight of what parts of the economy will deliver service and how they will deliver that service. Our priority, therefore, is to restore the economic system (i.e., the game plan). Every business has a clearly defined business model, and it must be clear how it will deliver profits.

This strategy calls for a self-defence posture through the adoption of the "Uncommon Market Borders, Uncommon Political Borders" principle, or the concept of "our country, our markets." Until such time as there is a global political union, the destabilising nature of free trade will continue. As a result, nations must review the concept of free trade to reflect national freedom of choice. Consequently, after much research and analysis, I have come up with what I consider to be an economic and manufacturing blueprint that can help any nation emerge from an economic crisis. Below, I go into detail about that blueprint.

Strategic Repositioning

The existence of a person or nation state is about one's relationship with the environment. At the centre of all things is the person (or state). In this case, I elevate individuals to be represented by the state as a collective body of citizens. Its environment is the economic system that promotes life, through providing all the basic needs of a person such as health, food, shelter, and security. The nation's quality of life depends on the nature and supply of these factors. As man is at the centre of the environment, it follows that a good strategic positioning for Zimbabwe is a "people-centred, inside out" approach, originating from man and his environment.

This addresses two divergent positions. One school of thought focuses on attracting foreign investment as central to economic success, while another prioritises citizens as the springboard for economic success. The rabble conditions I've discussed show dependence on the citizens as the foundation. The inside-out approach is a natural progression based on the nucleus of man extending his influence into the world. The opposite is an "outside-in" approach, an "egg economy," which is seemingly strong on the outside but crumbles as soon as the shell is removed. Before 1980, Zimbabwe's economy thrived on the bedrock of the white population. When they left, there was an economic meltdown. Excessive dependence on foreigners is unsound. Instead, a solid economy should be founded on the bedrock of its people, with foreigners augmenting that economy, not leading it.

The second layer of positioning is that the people should live in an environment that is able to sustain life. National leadership should provide such a habitat, where all five factors of production are present. They should work to improve the quality of the factors. Figure 7 shows the right relationships between a nation and its economic environment.

Figure 7: Typical Positioning of People inside Factors of Production

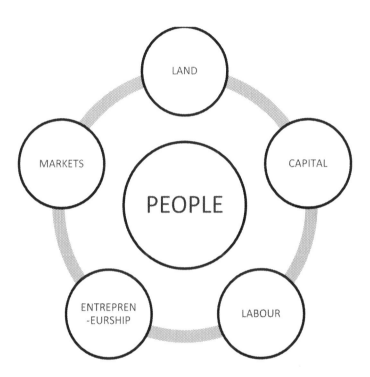

Meanwhile, figure 8 shows the right relationship between the people, the nation, and the international environment. It follows a process or sequence, with the people being the main actors in the nation's engagements with the environment. The domestic environment should be prioritised over international engagements. Violating these relationships leads to economic crises. When international corporate rights take precedence over national interests, it becomes nothing more than economic plunder. Defining and agreeing on who gets to be at the centre of the "egg"–the beneficiaries of the economic environment–is important. In this case, the economic system must always exist for its people.

Figure 8: Strategic Relationship between People and Their Environment

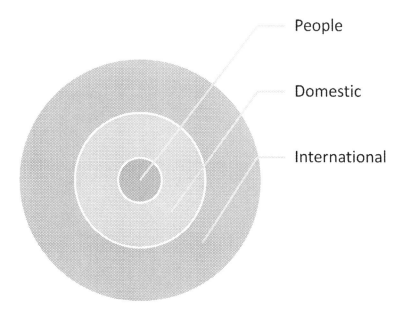

People

Domestic

International

The economic system will refresh itself by allowing the inward and outward flow of international factors of production without destroying its basic structure. Leadership must not abrogate responsibility and allow the relationships to become overgrown in an unbalanced way. The flow of such factors as international capital, labour, and entrepreneurs should be managed on the basis of a strategic fit to national interests. It cannot just be free movement and growth outside strategic review and sanctioning by the state. Everything that comes in or out affects the economic system in a positive or negative way; thus it is the state's responsibility to guard the system and to ensure it retains its ability to deliver value to the people. These factors should be based on free will. Free will means that a state should be able to assess, on behalf of its citizens, the extent to which the people benefit from international economic interaction. Conversely, the state will maintain its choices for import and export trade based on cost benefit analysis.

Figure 9 shows the right relationship and systems approach to economic management that Zimbabwe must pursue. It is the philosophy of the country. First and foremost, the people must believe in creating products for themselves as an essential function of an economic system. The priority is for a self-sustaining system, which requires the nation to develop its own capabilities to meet its needs. The system should allow for the distribution of surpluses and shortfalls through relationships with the outside world. However, the outside world should not replace the domestic system so that the system itself is crippled. The idea is not disconnection but rather healthy coexistence.

Figure 9: Typical Domestic-Based Supply System

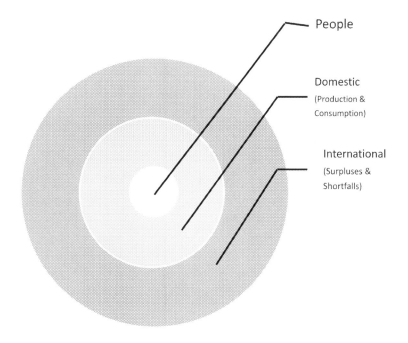

People

Domestic
(Production &
Consumption)

International
(Surpluses &
Shortfalls)

Restructuring and National Repositioning

After the strategic repositioning and alignment of the people, their nation, and the international community, it follows that there has to be a restructuring and realignment of internal systems to reflect this strategic focus. The key strategic issues that will need to be addressed are discussed below:

a. **Control of the Factors of Production.** This requires that the nation be in full control of the land, capital, labour, entrepreneurship, and market factors of production, focusing on their availability, maintaining their accessibility, and enhancing their quality as part of the growth and improvement process.

b. **The Restoration of an Economic System in the Country.** All the factors of production in the country need to be reviewed and reorganised. A systems mentality will ensure that productive assets be organised to serve domestic interests first, before they can serve or be served by the outside world. An economic system must be so organised that it can be self-existing and self-sustaining. This is the model that "miracle economies" have followed.

c. **Redefining Roles of Industry.** Industry, being a vital part of the economic system, must play its primary role by creating goods and services needed to satisfy domestic needs and consumption, with surpluses and shortfalls being traded with the international community. There should be no undue pressure to consume beyond the capabilities of the nation, to the extent that it harms itself with uncontrolled imports.

d. **Reorganising the Primary and Processing Industries.** Industry must be organised into primary processing industries, which must provide the raw materials needed by secondary producers and manufacturers to produce goods for the nation. That will require that there be a system of delivering goods to the people. The system must begin with mining and agriculture as primary industries, building into secondary processing and manufacturing industries. Strict protection of the sequence is important, because a system ceases to function if steps are skipped. This system must be jealously guarded. Unless primary processes have failed to supply to the system, duplication through the importation of processed products is wasteful and renders the primary industries themselves redundant. For example, if farmers fail to provide wheat in the country, it is good to import wheat and feed it through the system, from primary to secondary processing (in this case, through the milling industry to bakers and the retail networks). However, the current system is wasteful, because bakers import flour directly (and some retailers even bake directly); this bypasses the milling companies, which are vital parts of the system, and reduces their profitability.

e. **Reorganising Commerce and Trade.** Commerce and trade policies will have to be reviewed. Commerce is part of the local economic system, designed to play the role of distributing goods and services produced by the system first, then dealing with surpluses and shortfalls in the outside world. When commerce abandons its role in the system or business model, it ceases to be part of the system. Its primary role is to take from its industry and distribute to the people; its secondary role is to take from within or outside to augment shortfalls. That conceptual shape must be maintained by economic policy. Trade policies must be reviewed to restore the state's right to make strategic choices in the interests of all the people. Giving children blank chequebooks to spend on behalf of the family violates the strategy and control function of the nation's economic system.

f. **Finance and Banking Reforms Will Need to Be Put in Place.** Financial management is sorely needed to keep the national trade in balance and to align spending priorities with wealth creation through productivity. Banking institutions must support and promote industrialisation. Domestic financial institutions should be protected from failure by eliminating the performance risks of companies through the control of markets.

g. **The State Needs Its Own Currency for Internal Trade.** Foreign currency should be for import trade only. The present situation, where domestic trade is carried out in foreign currency, is wasteful and more so, where imports exceed exports, creates liquidity crises. Restoring a national currency will enable the Central Bank to manage the country's money supply. The introduction of a local currency will work well alongside a commitment to balancing trade.

Figure 10: Typical Domestic-Driven Economic System

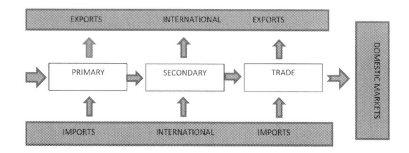

Realignments and Adjustments to Domestic Policies

The change in the country's positioning calls for a realignment of policies and practices in the economy, as follows:

a. **Imports and Exports.** Imports into the country should be managed so that they do not crowd out local production, while at the same time allowing some level of imports designed to give maximum benefits to citizens. Specific policies include:

(a) Prioritisation of productive assets such as machinery and raw materials not available in the country.

(b) Protecting local industries against destabilising imports. Since the economy should be domestically oriented, importing cheaper wheat when it is locally available would harm the primary industry of agriculture. Price goals should be subordinated to local productivity goals.

(c) Technology and price competitiveness can decommission an industry overnight, before it has run its full life cycle. The country will carry out technology impact assessments on the entire economic system.

(d) Publish national import priorities. Where imports are delegated to citizens, a national priority list should be published. This priority list should follow the pattern of productive assets, followed by infrastructure and consumption. Incentives should be put in place to guide behaviour.

(e) Monitoring and licensing the import of nonessential items. Where trade is balanced, there should be no need to control. However, since imports will be classified in terms of productive and nonproductive, the state should regulate nonproductive imports to influence the balance of trade.

b. **Leveraging Exports for Capital.** Export earnings, mostly from mineral resources, should be deployed to productive sectors. This can be achieved via the policy of managing foreign currency reserves and the import authorisation system. The deployment of foreign currency to productive sectors has the effect of import substitution and stabilising markets.

c. **Authorised Exports.** There is no need to export maize, only to import it back into the country again, unless there are clear and defined economic benefits. Exports should be based on the country's surplus production. Controls on the export of strategic grains should be put in place.

Strengthening the Factors of Production

As discussed earlier, the quality of the factors of production matters greatly to a nation's economic health. If citizens are blocked in their access to these factors, there will be no economic progress. The following policy adjustments will be necessary to enhance the quality of Zimbabwe's factors of production.

a. **Land.** There is need for a flexible policy to unlock land as capital, by freeing beneficiaries and owners to form partnerships, joint ventures, or transfer rights to their ninety-nine-year leases to other citizens. This will increase the availability of and access to idle land for beneficiaries, so it can be put to productive use.

b. Capital. Capital must be prioritised to develop local economies. The following policies and practices of raising capital should be put into place.

(a) Billions of dollars' worth of mothballed plants and machinery can be resuscitated, as a way of unlocking investment capital before spending a dollar from outside. These plants can then raise their own capital for improvements and technology updates. Other countries have dismantled aging production plants and redeployed them in other regions less prone to high competition.

(b) The country can further improve its capital position through savings from wasteful imports.

(c) Zimbabwe will have to leverage export earnings to raise domestic investment capital. This policy will multiply earnings and accelerate wealth accumulation.

(d) The country will need to attract foreign direct investment capital. To attract this capital, the investor will need to be incentivised with profits from guaranteed exclusive markets that will offer a credible return on investment.

(e) Zimbabwe's capital can be managed more efficiently by eliminating unnecessary investment duplications based on prioritising the profit interests of individuals. The telecommunications sector, for example, is one industry attracting unnecessary duplication, wasting millions in foreign exchange. But the country could also increase access to investment information by publishing a directory of current and existing investments and capacities, so that, as much as possible, investors can identify and invest in supply gaps, avoiding the waste of unwarranted, cut-throat competition. The number of players can be reduced and interested parties can participate through shares of listed entities. There is much duplication that can be eliminated.

c. Labour.

(a) Education and training should continue to be improved, but education should increasingly recognise industrial experience and achievements as qualifying criteria towards university certification.

(b) The Internet has increased access to the world's best practices in everything. Greater access to the Internet and "how-to" training programmes should be accorded to employees, which will accelerate learning and growth to world class levels.

(c) The policy of "markets for domestic companies first" should be adopted to allow novices to grow proficiencies through practice. The creation of employment as a result of pro-markets policies is an important tool for developing human capital, in that it allows for safe experimentation and experience building. Besides, increases in employment levels are synonymous with increased admissions to learning institutions. By reducing unemployment rates of upwards of 80 per cent, the impact on increased learning and growth will be great.

(d) Skills building. Practice makes perfect. The policy of doing it yourself will help build local proficiencies, knowledge, and skills. Government will need to adopt a policy of confidence with its people. Trust them with projects even if they do not do well at first. Zimbabwe's scientists, engineers, and consultants must be given contracts ahead of foreigners. That way, their capabilities can only increase.

(e) Attracting skills from the Diaspora. There must be a campaign that provides incentives for skilled citizens to return from abroad with new production ideas and projects. They could be guaranteed access to capital and domestic markets in much the same way as foreign investors.

(f) The nation will need to craft effective policies to strengthen health monitoring against debilitating diseases, such as HIV and cancers, currently affecting the labour force. In particular, policies must strengthen disclosure, accountability, and access to early treatment. Better economic management should improve health delivery services.

d. Entrepreneurship Development. The level of training and experience in entrepreneurship in Zimbabwe is already high due to the harsh conditions the country has already experienced. Entrepreneurs may be waiting for the right conditions to exist before they display their genius. However, the following policies will help unleash entrepreneurship more quickly.

(a) Entrepreneurship development policies will involve all the measures the government will take to provide easy access to productive factors (i.e., land, capital, labour, and markets). Where markets are serviced by imports, the government must always ensure there is space for entry by local entrepreneurs, by providing deliberate market gaps as "stretch" opportunities to encourage investment into those markets serviced by imports.

(b) State management of risks to entrepreneurs. When an entrepreneur has taken the risk to invest, the state should nurture his development by eliminating "bugs" in the form of superior foreign competition. Too much risk kills investment. Government should monitor the business failure rate and encourage investment. If only 10 per cent of all manufacturing start-ups ever succeed, then what is the point of risking capital and reputations in a local market?

(c) Control/manage the pace of technology changes. This can help manage risk and protect capital accumulation for the entrepreneur by stabilising markets and preventing bugs.

(d) Empowerment. The state will come up with policies to assist entrepreneurs, including providing for government guarantees on loans where necessary. Small Business Administration financing must be set up to support entrepreneurs. Government should consider loan grants for proven achievers. There should be access to venture capital, and inventors should be given grants to nurture their inventions into products.

(e) Trade fairs and exhibitions. The government can deliberately set aside a fund designed to incentivise foreign exhibitors to bring in and exhibit light industrial machinery and tools. Exhibitions are a good place to "pollinate" citizens with technology and ideas for production.

(f) Motivation. The government must motivate entrepreneurship through the reward of profit by guaranteeing markets. It can also directly motivate by bestowing honours and awards for industrial performance, giving prominence to those citizens who excel in these areas.

(g) Seeding of technology. The government should attract foreign investors and foreigners with new technical competencies by leveraging investment policies and immigration rules. Foreigners with special skills and certain capital thresholds should be incentivised to settle in the country.

(h) Entrepreneurship can also be developed through the introduction of controlled imports. Competitive imports are not altogether bad, so long as they will be used to immunise local industry and to set benchmarks for technology trends. Government should not ban imports altogether, but rather control the quantity of imports.

e. **Markets.** The fifth factor of production needed for a successful domestic economy must be created and preserved by the state. The following measures should be applied:

(a) The nation should monopolise markets in a selection of industries: agricultural produce, food manufacturing, clothing and textiles, plastic engineering, engineering products, construction, automobiles, and selected high tech products that are manufactured locally, such as refrigeration equipment, air conditioners, electrical appliances, and cables. In these industries, markets must be carefully managed to ensure that they are preserved and nurtured for growth.

(b) Production companies should be registered to determine the direction and need for markets for locally produced products.

(c) The introduction of new technology should be controlled to evaluate the degree to which they will destabilise existing industrial competitiveness.

(d) The importation of primary and semi-processed goods for local value addition and finishing should be introduced. This applies to trucks, buses, plants, and machinery.

(e) Imports should be controlled and licensed.

(f) The number of vehicle brands should be reduced, creating markets for local assembly. Such companies as Willowvale Mazda Motor Industries and Quest Motors should be encouraged to increase volumes of assembled cars, to compensate for a freeze on the import of second-hand cars.

(g) Retail chains should be required to give shelf space to local products (except where there are shortages). Foreign retail companies that exist solely for the sake of warehousing international products should be barred from entering local markets.

(h) Foreigners should not be allowed to participate in retail businesses.

f. Monetary Policy.

(a) Reintroduce the local currency.

(b) Legislate mandatory balancing of trade by the government.

(c) Sanction and monitor investments in nonproductive (from a balance of payments point of view), high capital, high maintenance projects.

(d) Control the movement of capital via limits and authorisation criteria by banks.

Adjustments

Systems View. There is a need to adjust the thinking of national economic planners so that they can adopt a systems view of the economy. Every aspect of the economy must be well coordinated to deliver economic success for the nation. The system should be like a gun, consisting of many parts and yet all functioning flawlessly to serve one purpose. Contradictions within the system must be eliminated.

Process View. There has to be a process view of economic delivery, beginning with primary processing to secondary processing, following through to commerce and international trade, as the components of the process. National consumer needs are to be provided for through the various stages of the process. Commerce should never be allowed to skip the process by parachuting in products from international markets, leaving primary and secondary processing industries without adequate amounts of business.

Process Approach to Industrialisation. The process of reaching world-class standards of industrialisation should be promoted. When leadership is impatient, it substitutes foreign goods to try to deliver economic growth for its own people, but this hardly ever empowers the people. However, a leadership that favours process thinking can confidently help its nation develop through a patient increase in skills and standards. Zimbabwe should adopt the process stages of imitation, improvement, improvisation, innovation, and invention, at the product, industry, and national levels of development.

When the five factors of production are combined, the climate is right for the continuous improvement philosophy to thrive. This thinking ensures that the citizens are involved and engaged in economic activity, in an environment that does not kill them.

The notion of smart sanctions as something less harmful than traditional full sanctions must change, to appreciate their deadly attack on the factors of production and the consequent paralysis of the entire economy.

The nation's view of free trade must be adjusted, given the principle that the superior power always defeats the inferior power. How inferior powers could earn their living under the circumstances should always be considered.

Regional Integration. There will be a need to reconsider the nation's headlong march towards regional markets integration, with special consideration to its competitiveness. Before integration, corporate Zimbabwe should be given the litmus test of first trying to penetrate the South African markets. If it succeeds, then it is ready for full integration.

National Interests. The nation will have to fully adjust to the idea that its vital national interests are those factors that promote the enjoyment of life by all citizens. Agreement on national interests is the only way to fortify the nation's democracy.

Ending the Financial Crisis. The idea that financial crises will somehow end through bailouts without addressing competitiveness factors will have to change. To simply give away money without addressing market forces is like pumping money into a bottomless pit. Every nation knows that profitable companies repay their debts. While market globalisation has taken place, in the absence of political integration, each country must view its economic system as independent and self-existing.

Secondly, each country must decide on how its economic system will connect to the world; how it will give or receive from the world.

Until such time when interstate economic rivalry is eliminated, and cooperation and mutual dependency are embraced as part of a one-world economic system, each nation must retain its right to self-defence by protecting its economic system and being at liberty to make its own rational and scientific choices on import and export trade.

A Final Word

I would like to thank you for reading about my worldview. This book encapsulates what I have learned, and I have shared this knowledge with you. I have given you my position honestly and without favour to any nation or political party. If in the process I have ruffled some feathers, that is exactly what I wanted to achieve: to stimulate thought and hopefully get everybody to make some adjustments to the truth. I have learnt that the truth is stubborn. You ignore it at your own peril.

My sole objective is to advance the interests of peoples all over the world through the experiences of the tiny nation of Zimbabwe. Never before have the interests of the world converged in one place than in the current need for economic progress. The economic risks are high, and not even the BRICS countries are safe. They will need to listen or else they too will be caught out in the open. These are lessons that any people struggling for economic well-being need reflect on, for the future lies not in "winner-take-all" policies, but in cooperation.

Every individual or nation has that spirit of corporate success. In Zimbabwe it is epitomised by that inner determination to succeed. It is what drives the nation to sacrifice. It is seen as the people sing their national anthems ahead of a great task, or as the thousands cheer their sporting heroes. At these moments, there is belief in the potential greatness of the nation, in the excitement that rises and falls depending on the results. We all love success, but now the world stands to win together.

Zimbabweans have every right to believe that the big tree that overshadows them can be cast away. They can rise up and shine. Just like those companies with juicy markets rose, they too can rise given the same juicy market conditions. Here is a blueprint that presents the hope of the "Rabble Effect," which promises that out of the rabble of Zimbabwe can rise a nation that will take its place among the industrialized nations of the world. They should not be afraid of change. Even if the rabble looks like they are going backwards. Just as one needs a deeper foundation for a skyscraper; creation, production and use of own products (zim-zhongs) is the beginning of industrial advancement.[47]

The foundations are there. The economy is ready for a mighty takeoff. And I can hear the distant echoes of the nation's victory song, "Yave Nyama Yekugocha, Baya Wabaya," meaning, "It's a done deal" (literally, "It's already braai meat, cut and cut"). If you doubted your destiny, there lies in this song, the passion and the promise.

It can be done!

---

47   David Chiweza, *HIV and AIDS: The Last Stand, the Total Strategy for the Annihilation of HIV and AIDS from the Rest of the World* (Harare: Ablecity (Pvt) Ltd., 1997).